CORRUPTION IN ITS BROADEST SENSE IS A SOCIAL PROBLEM
Elena Medina

Contents

Concept corruption 16

hierarchy degenerate systems 17

In horizontal corruption, agents collude , not found friend with friend subject to force relationships 18

reasons and Effects corruption 22

General problems, productive corruption: 23

problems, characteristic for Republic Belarus: 25

spheres raised risk corruption: 27

spheres existence base corruption: ... 27

Economic Effects corruption 29

Social Effects corruption 31

political Effects corruption 32

The main losses are due to the decisions made. bother agents to enter in degenerate relationship 33

Flat and indirect. 35

1.1. International and National date experienceSearch approaches with opposition corruption 35

1. Corporate basic knowledge: 41

2. political responsibility: 42

3. Extension opportunities participation civilian societies: 43

4. Competitive special sector: 43

5. Control public sector: 44

7. organized system vote persons over positions, dangerouswith point opinion corruption _............................. 47

1. organization customs operations:... 50

2. Charter to manage staff:............ 51

3. Internal culture:......................... 51

4. Investigation Crimes:................. 51

5. Control staff: 52

6. relationships with customers: 52

1.2. roads opposition corruption ... 55

HORSE 2001 year approved concept National security Res-public Belarus , in which? to fight with corruption determined in qualityone from priority instructions activities states 56

In 2000-2005 , the Republic of Belarus ratified a number of important agreements.the most important international conventions: the UN Convention against Corruption and transnational organized crime, Council of Europe Conventionrope about judicial and civil law responsibility back corruption. 57

Over prosecution assigned task coordinate deya- activities of all law enforcement and other government bodiesin to fight with corruption....... 59

- planning and Coordination activities law enforcementtelny and other to indicate, to declare sizes over to fight with corruption; 62

system national measures to fight with corruption: 62

principles to fight with corruption: ... 65

2.1. Meaning and role need Internationalcooperation in to fight with corruption 67

- spherical program against corruption UN. 68

- common opinion UN against corruption. 69

2.2. common opinion UN against corruption... 71

2) improved administrative and regulatory mechanisms for warnings corruption ;... 74

4) developed legal provisions for confiscation of funds, and Real estate, Acquired in conclusion corruption ; . 74

2.3. common opinion Council Europe 76

▪ active bribe National to indicate, to declare locationany person (Art. 2nd); 78

▪ active and passive bribe in

private sector (Art. Art. 7, eight); 78

personal quality or in composition body legal face, which? forni-mom leader location in legal face _ by: 80

2.4. Civil Law Agreementresponsibility back corruption 84

- legal Force transactions ; 86
- taking proof ; 86
- International cooperation 87

2.5. Twenty principles Council Europe over to fight with corruption 87

Twenty principles of the Council of Europefor to fight against corruption 88 corruption guilty 88

11. Ensuring that appropriate audit procedures are developed hunting with movements to indicate, to declare Services and public sectors 90

13. guarantee, What system public responsibilitytakes into account the consequences of corrupt behavior public officers... 90

18. Encourage Research over corruption _ 91

2.6. Activity International organizationsover to fight with corruption.. 92

3.1. Experience in developing formulation approachesfight corruption strategies over International 100

3.2. Experience development and application strategies opposition corruption in East Europe and Asia. 105

3.3. Tasks Research and diagnosis corruption 107

3.4. International instruments Research corruption 110

Independent courts should have capability endure 121

3.5. National instruments Research

corruption..124

4.1. role institutions Rights in opposition corruption.........................126

4.2. courts and corruption..............129

4.3. law enforcement sizes and corruption..133

4.4. political corruption and roads opposition he is 136

hour political corruption and dimension fee, and myself her...........137

Because the public interest is higher for social systemsprivate , then violations for personal gain no yourself Behave political corruption _

140

4.5. problems opposition political corruption.. 141

4.6. Sort Management corruption 156

4.7. Corruption and citizens. Corruption and business..................... 157

4.8. Ways to combat administrative corruption Management corruption - most Widespread opinion................. 163

which? and should hard. 165

Economic Effects manifestations corruption:... 168

Social Effects manifestations corruption :.. 169

political Effects manifestations corruption: 170

5.2. Vote tools 171

5.3. Practical experience in development and implementation fight corruption strategies in Republic Belarus 176

Regulator legal actions Minister Republic Belarus: 178

5.4. Place and role higher sizes executive 191

For increase competence to indicate, to declare to manage 192

5.5. The place and role of mass media

in application fight corruption Events 197

HORSE system quantity undertaken in opposition and to fightcorruption, established by the state and must be observed moral, ethical and legal principles adopted in society,only predetermining their civilized forms opposition corruption, however and public support in Generally. 199

5.6. role business and public organizations 201

One of the important issues determining success in the field of wrestling with corruption a to create priority instructions combat. 205

5.7. Corruption in sphere Education 208

5.8. Corruptio in sports................... 211

Concept corruption

how also none complicated social phenomenon, also corruption immortality available the only canonical definition. Sociologists, management professionals, economists, lawyers and simply citizens different interpret This concept.

sociologists , allegation What corruption This "refusal from expected mill darts behaviour partner side representatives authorities for the sake of illegal personal benefits." A lot expression going out and too much narrow (corruption maybeto be and in special companies), and too much wide.

believe that **"corruption in its broadest sense is a** social **problem** . phenomenon, striking public apparatus to manage, expression in Once upon a time-position of power, deliberate use of state and municipality officers, other executives girl to indicate, to declare functions, her formal provisions, situation and the authority of the position held for selfish purposes for personal purposes extinguishing or in group out."

Within the scope of corruption in article 1 of **the Law of the Republic of Belarus of July 20 2006 No. " On anti-corruption " for 165-Z** , "... intentionaluse by a public official or equivalent a person in an official position or a foreign official and related opportunities, illegal obtaining property or other benefits in the form of services, patronage promises of benefits and bribery for himself or third parties public official or an equivalent person or any other personodd attendant by providing

them with property, or other benefit in the form of a promise of service, protection, advantage this public duty for them or for third parties. foreign or equivalent person or foreign official acted or avoided doing while performing they service (labor) tasks."

hierarchy degenerate systems

Hierarchical **classification corruption over types customers** (rice. 1.1)**divided into two categories** - corruption accompanied by interaction With non- **official clients in this incarnation tsami,** and **customers _ participating** third side in degenerate dei- movements, **in quality formal persons** . First event in your name **extrinsic**

corruption over types customers

In decreasing and **increasing corruption, intermediary and** customer directly or **simultaneously in** agency relations through intermediate principles, ie. **part of the same hierarchy chemical chain. With top-down corruption from the client side** , ie . face, to bribe **, that is, is a higher official** . rachis With increased **corruption** by the client , ie . bribe giver ku, **a formal face, found below** in the hierarchy.

In horizontal corruption, agents collude , not found friend with friend subject to force relationships .

Mixed internal corruption , **mutual existing corrupt officials with each other** (in different combinations) taniyah) **in different** from listed above,

relationships .

An example of this is interactive **corruption. networks - groups of corrupt officials** united in the **long run for extraction selfish benefits** from his position.

External corruption is conditionally divided into **two** large **groups** . First - **house corruption.** HORSE How are you today? situation in quality customers behavecitizens, to enter in interaction with strength. Here valid degenerate-time in to indicate, to declare universities and medical institutions, military commissars and hunting-inspections, institutions social make sure and sections militia.

Second Group - **business corruption** _ in which? in quality customers joyful-representatives of non-governmental organizations (legal entities) are walking. This May to be representatives business, public organizations or other other non-government organizations. The important thing is mutualacting with formal persons and to enter with to them in degenerate opportunities,these representatives defend the interests of their organizations. for example, if The owner of the restaurant was stopped by the traffic inspector on his way home in the evening, then bribe last should to be assigned with local corruption. If one he is same the owner of the restaurant bribes the sanitary-epidemiological representative or other Species supervision, who did come in restaurant for next control OS-moth, back then How are you today? deal valid with business corruption.

Business corruption can do, in mine order, **Share over spheres** they belong relating to organizations. can talk about corruption in Trade, oil and gas production, science, Education, MEDIA, journalism, politics, International relationships and etc.

Available special medicine customers, degenerate opposite whose behavior with authorities is difficult to attribute to any of the following: the two types of corruption mentioned above. These are the representatives of the criminal Peace. To this end, **a special kind of external corruption is a crime.** In this case, the **customer representative of the underworld** and its **corrupt interaction To compete** with an agent is **to secure the interests of the criminal** . **physical**

activity. Representation that provides the picture information to a criminal group about the progress of their criminal investigation lenia, including judicial corruption.

corruption according to its types, low **high** and **top corruption.** The basis of distinction is **level Number of decision makers and scale** of decision making **we are X decisions** by themselves. And The second criterion is more important.

For example, an official - a deputy minister or chief ka management can appoint using their official positions. low position in ministry or someone's department distant relatives. Neither base refers to corruption. But if again for assistant secretary or other low-ranking official bribery will affect the outcome of a major government contract, such rupee should valid with apical Should Sign and he is truth,that it is often difficult to correctly classify the manifestation of corruption. VAT and attributed to one of its specified types. This happens especially often in Sound situation, if corruption there you go in kleptocrat system.

reasons and Effects corruption

Corruption is a complex and diverse phenomenon. Therefore, also The multiple possibilities of causes are varied. Therefore, it is impossibleThey are prone to the fact that a one-sided view can bring a one-sided view of the problem. meaningful answer. Only a multifaceted analysis of the phenomenon can illuminate its inner essence, scale, dynamics, structure and therefore to indicate over instructions opposition and fight against he is.

corruption, he is scale, specificity and dynamics - **conclusion** general over-lytic, social and economic **problems** none countries. Bond Me too- I am waiting corruption and productive he is problems - two sided. With onehand, these problems aggravate corruption a to them decision maybe path-to reduce corruption. On the other hand, scale**corruption protects and aggravates problems** transition period _ **Me too-shakes to them decision** . From here follows, What, Before everything, **decrease and Boundary- Corruptnenaybe cured** by simultaneously solving the **generated problems** . **to give he is**

problems ; Latter, - **decision** these **problems encourages pro- opposition corruption** over everybody instructions.

Common problems that lead to corruption include: rye, in the modernization phase, experienced, transition period from extreme centralization to socialization oriented market economy. Not all are Res- characteristic. Belarusian people, but the enumeration of these problems allows us to understand them. affect over problem corruption Generally.

General problems, productive corruption:

1. Difficulties overcome heritage totalitarian period.

2. Economic to reject and political instability.

3. under development and mistake legislation.

4. inefficiency institutions authorities.

5. weakness civilian society, separation societies from authorities.

6. not rooted democratic political traditions.

7. under development legal consciousness population and her knowledgeablens.

8. Appearance conditions democracy also absence in society peoples, talented competently to them perceive and benefit for general good.

9. unscrupulous competition over established markets between-people systems producing and consumption.

10. availability politically conditioned systems "couple standard-comrade" to countries and manufacturers.

11. Not entrance countries in structure WTO.

12. The perception in some circles that democracy is tolerant Contrary to understanding it as a system in which all elements take mutual responsibility, police officers societies friend former friend in process movements with unified

targets.

13. Deficiencies in the economic feasibility analysis system, profitability and completeness of control over its implementation and repayment to indicate, to declare projects.

14. Disadvantages in work control to indicate, to declare organs.

15. Disadvantages in system patent and licensed activities,protection intellectual property.

16. Disadvantages in system education literate managers homeowner-natural mechanism in a market economy.

17. Insufficient transparency in sphere financing and worker-news public institutions and political parties.

problems, characteristic for Republic Belarus:

1. weakness judicial systems.

2. blockage legal spheres legal documents.

3. High school dynamics Changes in legislation.

4. under development legal consciousness population.

5. partially preserved orientation of law enforcement officers and their representatives is to protect the "interests of the state". festival to citizens.

6. The sometimes encountered custom of subordinating officials, horse, a instruction to the boss.

7. development foreign economic Links in conditions globalizationand established international Market separation labor.

8. export oriented Market producing.

9. Disadvantages in work design organizations.

Rapid changes are taking place in the economic field, new unusual areas and forms of business activity. Competence decision making ensures the efficiency of economic activity news, a investment climate effects over external picture statesin general, ultimately - about living conditions in the country. why is it harder It is only institutions of power that will adapt. This is the most felt growth corruption.

spheres raised risk corruption:

1. Customize to indicate, to declare Real estate.

2. To apply budget and distribution budget source of money.

3. banking sphere.

4. lobbying in legislative organs.

5. law enforcement sizes and economic crime.

spheres existence base corruption:

1. Residential and partner sphere.

2. law enforcement organs.

3. taxes and customs fees.

4.   call over military service.

5.   Health care.

6.   Education.

7.   control and supervision activity.

8.   permissive and licensed sphere.

Corruption in the Republic of Belarus , as in many other countries ,of the problems that are tackled and related to the manifestation carried out systemic opposition. July immortality little, cause endure mogo relationships with he is a extremely weak conscious society he is immortality-Negative results. Due to the lack of knowledge of the citizensquestion Like this and disdain character degenerate coup over communityin and to indicate, to declare in Generally. What naturally aggravates he is affect. Important, What-if the whole society not only recognizes and determines the manifestations of harmony,rupee, however and immortality allowed can be tolerance behaviour with he is. For it was to want no oneclearly think manifestations corruption Total only as one from Species crimes inherent only in the immoral acts of individuals, persons with powers. Undoubtedly, corruption rotting affect over all side life society.

To get a more complete picture of the impact of corruption on various environments other aspects of the life and activities of society and the state, executing some of its negative consequences in one way or another located in modern conditions on the territory of nearby countries, Like this and far away.

Economic Effects corruption

1. The shadow economy is expanding . which leads to a decrease tax revenues and weakening of the budget. As a result, the state the state is losing its financial leverage to manage the economy, social problems Because of default budget obligations.

2. The competition mechanisms of the market are violated because then the winner is not the competitive but the noncompetitive. they can get legal help. This causes a reduction in the effect competence Market and discredit opinions market competition.

3. slow down appearance effective special productions and owners, primarily due to violations during privatization time, a also artificial bankruptcies.

4. Ineffective used budget say _ in special - in the distribution of government orders and loans. More than that aggravates budget problems countries exposed corruption.

5. rising due to "overall costs" **dov"** .AT to suffer consumer.

6. getting worse investment climate , and, from here, immortality solving-has problems overcome recession producing, updates mother background-beat. hour agents Market visible unbelief in capability authorities To upload,control and follow honest regulations Market relationships.

7. Corruption in civil society organizations is on the rise organizations. This leads to a decrease in the efficiency of their work and to betray, reduced efficiency economies Generally.

Social Effects corruption

1. distracted from targets public development facilities, has huge volumes . This exacerbates the budget crisis. older sister, decreasing capability authorities to make a decision social Problems.

2. still and increases Real estate inequality _ bad-ness bigger parts population. continues unfair redistribution girl source of money in use narrow groups back Control most sensitive layers population.

3. Law is being discredited as the main regulatory tool. In the minds of the people of the **life** of the state and society , the idea of citizens' vulnerability as before crime, Like this and in front authorities.

4. There is a strengthening and expansion of organized preliminary preparations. stupnosti due to corruption by law enforcement.

Organized crime merging with corrupt groups- further developed with the help of authorities and entrepreneurs. Entrance with political power and opportunities laundering from money.

5.   Increasing social tension , decreasing level development economy threat political stability in country.

political Effects corruption

1.   national   **targets.** development with to ensure sovereignty these or other clans.

2.   decreases   self-confident with power _ growing he is estrangement from society. July most are placed under threatening none he is socially important projects.

3.   The country's prestige in the international arena is falling, the threat is increasing he is economic and political insulation.

4.   Political competition is reduced and disrespected . Gra- citizens become disillusioned with the values of democracy. decay occurs democratic institutions.

5. Risk of collapse of development-based democracy rises scenario parish with authorities dictatorships over wave fight against corruption.

Should Sign, What in Generally **economic casualties from corruption lots wider and Deeper How This like that with point opinion simple he ispredictions as Total quantities bribe** - Price:%s, which? pay specialfaces or companies corrupt officials or politicians.

The main losses are due to the decisions made. bother agents to enter in degenerate relationship .

For example, an order received as a result of dishonest bidding paying an unscrupulous artist. Related losses more than worth the bribe that promotes injustice stnoe decision tender commission.

actual **losses significantly exceed those estimated Trustworthy over basis Sound defined degenerate works and** completed **investigations** , their results (their order) May affect immortality defined degenerate relationships.

Economic casualties from corruption Share over two categories:

Flat and indirect.

Direct losses - shortfall in budget revenue due to corruption and **inefficient spending of budget funds** for the same reasons on foot. **Indirect casualties** - general **downgrade competence economy** _ conjugate with corruption.

1.1. International and National date experience Search approaches with opposition corruption

Corruption has been the problem of every state throughout history. the logical existence of this institution. world experience it seems The fight against corruption is just as rich. However, it is not. In no way each one to indicate, to declare generally perceived corruption as problem and front proud to fight him. Corruption detected in some countries like something natural. For example, in ancient

India Kautilya, chief Advisor to Emperor Chandragupta Maurya (321 - 297 BC), listed Lil in Arthashastra (an ancient Indian political and economic examination) 40 Species allowances officers to indicate, to declare Income.

In other states of antiquity, corruption was simply necessary. for the ruling regime. The unmatched stability of the patriarch The ancient Chinese bureaucracy had its roots in efficient mechanisms. atomization of bureaucracy, prevention of steady gathering of officialscompanies that could oppose the emperor and Night and day After all keep also that power.

One of these mechanisms was the financial dependence of the authorities. ka not from the imperial salary, but from his ability to squeeze out of the emperor- maximum income from their subjects, including their own personal interests. This inevitably turned officials into an easily vulnerable violation of the law. horses with all the consequences - fear of exposure chenya, opportunity "Castle him hook."

Bribery has since become illegal in Russia In the times of the incentive decrees of Peter I, it remained one of the means comrade belongings public deals among the political elite and all other weight Russian officials.

Wide application development and applications fight corruption programs are characteristic of the more natural modernity, because basis development societies a Setup over reorganization Peace, -

so-called "social engineering", which is often a branch of a engineering fight corruption.

One of the first successful experiences in the fight against corruption tion to be think **reform to indicate, to declare service** _ which? it happened Done **in United States of America** in 1887.

corruption programs that emerged in the twentieth century In **the East** , especially in China, a **completely different versatility** . Not so, since its main predecessors are destruction with degenerate practitioner, how many corruption

accumulated resistance experience , actively opposition corruption **Share**

over two sufficient general **groups**. The group includes measures to combat **external manifestations of corruption (bribery)** . special officers) with already existing corruption special nym corrupt officials. **second group** format quantity to fight with institute- rational preconditions for corruption , **potential Noah corruption** _ topics impersonal corrupt official in to who maybe, also immortality- which? conditions, turn into formal.

In practice, **the strategy of systematically eliminating the causes of corruption involves combating** certain corrupt officials and **The "war" label against corruption,** albeit in a fragmented form , **rowan bird** and **to eliminate the causes** .

The main focus in strategy development is elimination. reasons productive corruption a immortality over external manifestations How are you today? problems (events corrupt officials).

The variety of approaches to the systematic elimination of causes is great. can, in especially emphasize radical and temperate fans How are you today? strategies.

Various options available for anti-corruption strategies to show a variant of "anti-corruption institutionalism", day former extreme degree. HORSE none her format (Moreover cannot be performed)

"anti-corruption institutionalism" looks quite attractive Remarkably: the complexity of the approach looks believable and inspires confidence ness in success reforms.

HORSE back then same time, "enlightened" fight corruption institutionalism be aware limitation her programs frame "healthy societies", undercitizenship traditions and political competition, an independent judiciary really works subject and civil administration rationally and technically efficient effective. Other words fight corruption institutionalism and her

The strategy is only suitable for implementation with respect to established countries. forms of democracy (such as the Western European model) and its mom corruption For more their minimization.

Table 1.1 presents one of the possible classifications of countries. labeled

numbers opposite the following descriptions:

1. This set of strategies includes programs that apply to: covers the entire territory of the country and all or at least more public authorities. An example of such a strategy is the global fight corruption program, accepted central state.

2. This group includes programs that affect a partition, but spread throughout the country. There are enough examples of such strategies You are very nice. It is usually initiated within the institution itself and is mandatory. for local sections How are you today? departments.

3. This group contains programs that are valid for the entire region. It is a regional unit and affects a large number of state bodies in the region. torii of this region. Often, such anti-corruption strategies are initiated Have a large-scale influence on the initiative of the regional leadership and the work of the majority Lower government officials in the region. To scale and in- intensity of influence, they do not go beyond the boundaries of individual areas, zones, other units administrative-territorial (or local) division.

4. This group consists of native programs with the "dot" character. influential. A lot programs directed over opposition corruption at a specific government agency at the regional level. such an example Anti-corruption measures can be pilot or trial projects. opposition special types broken relationships in Concrete conditions.

Employees World Jar advanced "Unified You are very nice-aim strategy to fight with corruption", formed from five sections:

1. Corporate basic knowledge:

— institutionalization independent and productive judicial authorities;

— extension spheres movements parliamentarian control;

— security independence law

enforcement organs.

2. political responsibility:

— political competition, deserving trust politicalsky parties;

—   transparency in financing parties;

—   transparency procedures voting for voters;

—   task officers report Real estate, regulations, again- Walk question conflict they come out.

3.   Extension opportunities participation civilian societies:

—   guarantee freedom information;

—   to win rollers MEDIA.

4.   Competitive special sector:

—   restructuring monopolies with aim increase competitive started;

—   to reject obstacles entrance over market, related with necessity taking various permissions;

—   transparency Corporate to manage;

— increase Right business associations.

5. Control public sector:

— hiring over to indicate, to declare service over basis merit, venerablePayment labor officers;

— decentralization authorities;

— promotion transparency budget process for control- friction organs;

— increasing transparency in tax administration, opportunity for tax officials to tax arbitrarily privileges, simplification tax administration.

HORSE 2001 year advanced systemic **strategy, created special- stasis World Jar** substantially enriched. **HORSE he is** had **including** in the pastsome parts, such as the institutionalization of **a special anti- corrosion corruption sections, Adoption ethic codes,** need **from-logical programs over to fight with corruption** also to indicate, to declare purchase , a also **mobilization support hold reforms,** as partner side civilianDanish society, Like this and partner side political leaders.

In practice , **an example of a comprehensive struggle against .** tiv corruption **a fight corruption strategy Netherlands** _HORSE Generally, Dutch fight corruption strategy created in frameIt was considered a strategy to eliminate the causes of corruption. in their approach there is and elements "war" strategies against corruption.

The anti-corruption system in the Netherlands includes: english procedural and Corporate quantity:

1. Continuous reporting and publicity on discovery issues corruption and argument results - penalties back degenerate dei-

movements. Every year, the Minister of the Interior of that country, public back Results activities over to fight with corruption.

2. development systems tracing possible point to appear-acts of corruption in government and public institutions stations and tight control activities persons, found in these point.

3. **creating systems Right and responsibilities formal persons with know- holding them accountable for violating business ethics** , including corruption. This system also displays the code of conduct for correction. nyu violations committed.

4. **measurement mother punishment back degenerate action is- is-xia forbidden work in to indicate, to declare organizations and loss allsocial benefits provided** by the public service , for examplemeasures, pensions and social services. The penalty scale includes: in myself also fines and temporary suspension from yield responsibilities.

5. **In all important organizations** , for example - in ministries, **have-internal security services** , whose task is the registry office ihfatn ad dtefn of errors, intentional or accidental violations of the authorities festival existing Charter and relating to results lots violations.

6. **Government agencies want to promote positivity There is no action by the authorities** . The reward system aims to: in order to benefit the officer both materially and morally. work honest and efficient.

7. organized system vote persons over positions, dangerous with point opinion corruption _

8. Everything materials, related with degenerate movements mandatory **, if it** does not affect the national security system . name OK **to be accessible for the public** .

9. Every official has the right to receive information, to characterize her as with positive Like this and with negative side.

10. There is a special education system for civil servants, especially to explain the political and social harm of **corruption** and possible results of joining he is.

11. created system to indicate, to declare security over to fight with corruption medicine special police, have important forces to determine cases corruption.

12. Officials at all levels are required to record what is known. **corruption cases** and this information is sent to them through appropriate channels. transmitted in ministries internal works and justice.

13. Big role in to fight with **corruption Play facilities mass information** _ which? make public cases corruption and often to actualize to them immortality- dependant investigation. HORSE back then same time slanderous Messages Loss of plktrust and reputation of relevant resources information. July most is blocked in important degree, unanswered-Real estate in prepare disclosure materials.

such as **Israel** _ Corruption-free countries This is achieved along with similar ones. Measures implemented in the Netherlands, a tracking replay system to the ring possible degenerate movements.

This control is carried out by government agencies and private organizations. police departments, State Control Department independent of ministries and state authorities friends, and public organizations medicine "Chapters back purity Right- authority." These organizations to discover possible degenerate point, a inIf they are found, notify the investigating authorities. and received- no information should in compulsory OK to be brought former public sti. It is very important that these organizations are independent from the leadership of the ministries . adparmetwhxefimahendelcorruption . in controlAlso for the fight against corruption, which is a part of the Prime Ministry .It is mandated to continuously train the authorities on prevention. possible corrupt practices and various internal department Services over to fight back purity to indicate, to declare organs.

The media also plays an important role. According to one The politicians of this country are the most dangerous for its politics. career corruption allegations that may seem solid newspaper. It should be noted that **in Israel, important social benefits for the authorities and** their brutal **punishment when inflicted** weaponry **corruption, base corruption practically lost** .

National departmental anti-corruption programs Used to counter corruption in customs and taxes. government offices of various states. Anti-corruption use Strategies in these departments are sometimes determined by non-compliance with rules. Indicators for collection of taxes and fees. For example, tax reform **in Tanzania** administration, according to the Confederacy, began because of the fact This state's budget of Tanzanian industries 250 billion tanza lost as a result of corruption of tax officials nian shilling in 2000 – 2004

Anti-Corruption Strategy Model in Customs, **supplied experts International monetary fund, capital,** formed from six chapters:

1. organization customs operations:

— definition standards to indicate, to declare Services;

— separation functions and institutionalization systems checks and pro-weights;

— limitation optional forces Customs officers;

— computerization customs functions;

— minimization necessary information from traders.

2. Charter to manage staff:

— development code behaviour;

— definition corruption and related Crimes;

— to create systems sanctions.

3. Internal culture:

— development Corporate soul;

— development missions and targets customs.

4. Investigation Crimes:

— application mechanisms internal audit;

— conductive regular external audit;

− conductive random selective checks customs authorities;

− organisation sections have security;

− incentive special operators back information about formalcrimes;

− control declarations about Real estate officers.

5. Control staff:

− vote and promotion personnel based over principle meritand merit;

− rotation employee;

− sufficient level monetary fee;

− system prize.

6. relationships with customers:

− relaxation Entrance all customers with department actions;

− institutionalization independent systems appeal Answers.

Local universal program opposition degenerate- tion includes most various fight corruption programs. unite nyayuschimi factor in given situation serves lots collapsed coverage in the pastto them programs or strategies, - them immortality come out back frame one or many to them administrative-territorial (local) formations.

ver application available **two choice local anticorrosive** corruption **strategies The first is** a developed anti-corruption strategy. **He was personally accepted for execution by Botan and district** officials . Second- herd - regional strategy , **national** andThis is a pilot (trial) phase of national implementation. Noah (National) fight corruption strategies. Success or failure of the experiment has important consequences because Results adhere to the future nationwide strategy

Turning to the analysis of the technological aspects of regional developments universal anti-corruption programs, significant differences from the above mentioned national standards not grams Like this You are very nice. More meaning owner at that time, What over local level missing provides more opportunities to improve a set of anti-corruption measures or partial implementation of the measures adopted anti-corruption strategy. This is because **regional gram deals with a more homogeneous medium** . That's why wrestlers fear - Rpm gives you **more opportunities to** fine- **tune your strategy. under** real **needs** specific **region** .

Regional departments have **different anti-corruption strategies hope** more more **narrow orientation** . These to suggest application anti-corruption measures in one or more departments level administrative-territorial (local) Education.

Small **scale Events allows** , with one hand is to plan activities in **more** detail and **accurately,** and on the other hand , **To escape** unnecessary **resonance** over about strategy applied.

In addition, **regional department strategies substantial resources** like their larger counterparts , thereforeThe beginning of the development and implementation of an anti-corruption strategy is usually sufficient however only political will guides departments. By How are you today? reason in World implementing anti-corruption activities, numerous examples local department fight corruption strategies.

1.2. roads opposition corruption

No, as corruption has become a large-scale issue of our time. a single state regardless of its socio-economic and political status. logical devices, immortality owner absolute Him immunity.

signature in 2003 year **contracts organizations Unified Over-tion against corruption** and application opinions creation **international association**

The formation of anti-corruption institutions is the result of a deep awareness. spherical community serious danger results corruption.

Supporting and developing anti-corruption initiatives At the national, regional and international levels, **the Republic of Belarus Russia was one of the first** member states **to ratify the Convention time** UN against corruption.

HORSE **1997** year **accepted Live Republic Belarus "HE quantity to fight with organized crime and corruption** " nine years service building foundation fight corruption politicians states.

HORSE **2001** year approved **concept National security Res-public Belarus** , in which? to fight with corruption determined in quality one from priority instructions activities states .

The **first** specialized **State in 2002 _ program over strengthening to fight with corruption** over 2002 - 2006 years. HORSE Once Upon a Time - Improving the implementation of the organizational and legal measures of tiProgramWe **accepted rowing legislative actions fight**

corruption directed-information - Laws of the Republic of Belarus " **About civil service in the republic public Belarus ," oh declare physically persons Income, Real estate and resources monetary funds ", " oh quantity over prevention legalization of illegal and financially generated income english terrorist activity** ."

Decrees **of the President of the Republic of Belarus " On the issuance and the use of gratuitous (sponsored) assistance ", " About trust management of owned public officials participation shares (shares, rights) in legal funds of commercial organizations organizations** ", also a decree on the debureaucratization of the state donation apparatus, to streamline administrative procedureslead times degenerate action to indicate, to declare employees and others

In 2000-2005 , **the Republic of** Belarus ratified a number of important agreements. the most important international conventions: **the UN Convention against Corruption and transnational organized crime, Council of Europe Conventionrope about judicial and civil law responsibility back corruption.**

fulfillment they International obligations, a, also Thinking

a belated need to develop new alerting methods prevention and suppression of corruption, Republic of Belarus further forward Development fight corruption legislation.

July **2006** a new Law of the Republic of Belarus **"On the Struggle"corruption ."** This law establishes the legal foundations of the state. venous politicians in sphere to fight with corruption directed over protection Right

and citizens' freedoms from threats to the public interest. phenomenon corruption. Security productive activities to indicate, to declare military bodies, other government officials, and equal with he is persons, by warnings, identification, Suppressionand disclosure of crimes that create the conditions for corruption and corruption crimes, eliminate them results.

In accordance with the law, the fight against corruption, prosecutor's office, internal affairs and state security bodies sti , both independently and in **interaction with each other ,withhelp of**

state institutions and organizations as well as **citizens** Republic of Belarus.

to indicate, to declare sizes and other organizations compulsory to forward public sizes to apply to fight with corruption in- formation, related with truths testimony about corruption.

Over prosecution assigned task coordinate deya- activities of all law enforcement and other government bodies in to fight with corruption.

HORSE fit with **decree Minister Republic Belarus from 17 also-December 2007, republic, district and county coordination meetings** to fight crime and corruption . Coordination meetings are chaired by the relevant ministers. prosecutors. coordination **meetings has continually action- howling interdepartmental** bodies.

decision to fulfill the requirements of the law prosecution offices Republic Belarus, ministries internal works Republic of State Security Committee of the Republic of Belarus **approved Draft degenerate crimes**. With he is assigned:

1. theft by abuse formal forces.

2. Smuggling committed by an official to eat official powers.

3. legalization ("laundering") material values, Purchased by criminal means committed by an official using arrogance they formal forces.

4. financing terrorist activities, perfect formal face with using they formal forces.

5. Abuse of power or official authority greedy or other personal interest.

6. Inaction by official authority outside of power or self-interest Noah or other personal interest.

7. EXTREME authorities or formal forces, perfect fromselfish or other personal interest.

8. Service forgery.

9. Illegal participation in entrepreneurial activities. 10. Receipt

bribe.

11. Cottage bribe.

12. mediation in bribe.

13. Illegal wages by public officialsfoot device, immortality structure formal face.

14. Abuse of power, excessive force or inaction power stemming from selfish or other self-interest (military a crime).

As practice shows, the most common corruption mi Crimes has theft, abuse strength, formalforgery, taking and cottage bribe, taking illegal fee to indicate, to declare employees, immortality structure formal face. Over Share these compositions front steps give account almost 40 % from general numbers fixed corruption nyh Crimes, remainder in given dynamics practically yearly.

Based on the analysis of the practice of applying criminal law, recommendations of relevant government agencies for improvement. baptism legislation about the fight with corruption.

In general, the **fight against corruption is carried out in the Republic of Belarus. is based on the integrated implementation** of the **measures . consistent with common opinion UN** against corruption.

Mother from to them are:

— **criminological studies of corruption crimes Noah focus** in purposes describing reasons corruption, to them predictionsand the prediction of the development of the situation for timely adoption is effective quantity by warning corruption;

— planning and Coordination activities law enforcement telny and other to indicate, to declare sizes over to fight with corruption;

— **economic development and implementation blind- rupee** with elimination prerequisites he is existence.

system national measures to fight with corruption:

— planning and coordinating

the activities of government agencies gans and the other organizations over to fight with corruption;

— identification of special requirements as well as restrictions, managed over security monetary control in relationship to indicate, to declare

authorities to prevent manifestations of corruption tion and their identities;

— security legal arrangement activities to indicate, to declare military bodies and other organizations, government and public control and surveillance back How are you today? activity;

— improvement of the system of state organs, personnel work and procedures Answers Questions providing protection Right, freedom and legitimate areas of interest physically and legal persons;

— to get better violated Right, freedom and legitimate areas of interest fi physically and legal persons, liquidation damaging results guilty-no, create conditions for corruption, and degenerate Crimes;

— Establishment of legal prohibitions to distinguish between service other (business) duties and personal, group and other non-task areas of interest to indicate, to declare formal and equal with he is persons;

— Judgment in accordance with the provisions of official legislation The Belarusian people, in order of public servants and equally warranties and indemnities granted to them with respect to restrictions, established live "HE to fight corruption" and other legislator- telny actions of the republic Belarus in sphere fight against he is;

— withholding or otherwise providing financing financial support for the activities of state institutions and organizations by organizations from sources and in ways not prescribed by law. stvom Republic of Belarus;

— conductive criminological Research degenerate crime in purposes he is predictions and guess for describing prerequisites and reasons corruption, timely admission effective measures he is warning and prevention;

— anti-corruption and economic parcels to eliminate it reasons.

At the same time, the entire system of measures to combat corruption is based on: System of principles established by the state and accepted in society given wrestle, What provides he is competence.

principles to fight with corruption:

— Legality.

— Justice.

— equality all former by law.

— Promotion.

— inevitability responsibility.

— Personal guilty responsibility.

— humanism.

Everything This shows over availability in

Republic Belarus thin and Message-yanno improvement systems to fight with corruption. However important actualRUM success given to fight a need he is application immortality only law enforcement bodies. task room one for all guide-ditel, and in first order to indicate, to declare sizes and organizations, absolute ensuring the personnel cleanliness of the team, legal and moral cleaning everybody worker and, together with topics active inclusionin to fight with corruption Total civilian society.

LESSON 2nd. INTERNATIONAL LEGISLATION AND INTERNATIONAL VEHICLES PROVISIONS CORRUPTION

2.1. Meaning and role need International cooperation in to fight with corruption.

2.2. common opinion UN against corruption.

2.3. common opinion Council Europe about judicial responsibility back corruption.

2.4. common opinion about civil law responsibility back corruption.

2.5. Twenty principles Council Europe over to fight with corruption.

2.6. Activity International organizations over to fight with corruption.

2.1. Meaning and role need International cooperation in to fight with corruption

International cooperation is also considered one of the ways.standardization quantity to fight with corruption over legal level and as use - measures that are not definedinthe regulatory system International fight corruption Help. An example lots quantity May mud live « **Suggestions relatively International cooperation in about- crime prevention and criminal justice in the context of development** » 1990 g. **accepted** over 68. General Assembly meeting **General HUNGRY-United Nations examples**. International acceptance of such "Recommendations" organization was necessary because, as stated in this document, them: "...corruption between to indicate, to declare formal persons maybe flatten over

program has no potential effectiveness, make it difficult development and to create threatening for individual persons and groups persons".

Corruption exists in one form or another in all states, generally accepted its international character. Corruption in the international arena legal actions are defined as a global one problems in the field make sure international law and order.

The international community is trying to join forces in this case warnings and Suppression corruption. HORSE now time quantity over warning The prevention of corruption is presented in a number of international anti-corruption documents. twelve programs. Between mother given the following:

— spherical program against

corruption UN.

— declaration UN about to fight with corruption and bribe in International advertising operations.

— common opinion UN against corruption.

In the parliaments of all countries, they examine and generalize the experiences of both countries. friendship, international experience and international practice cooperation in the fight against corruption. For this purpose,International conferences within the framework of the Inter-Parliamentary Assembly Conferences and seminars on CIS countries, UN conventions and veta Europe over to fight with corruption.

International cooperation should help states develop work unified administrative and legal facilities for fulfillment of obligations undertaken in the field of prevention and suppression corruption in the civil service system. foreign experience to fight with corruption owner key meaning and continually Usedin National legislation.

United Kingdom a one from first countries, which? accepted back- con " **oh prevention corruption**." **United States of America** first accepted live

Corrupt Activities Abroad ". in **Hong** Kong in 1974 established commission over opposition corruption, which? carried out

"silence revolution" in society. An example productive to fight with corruption he is, a **operation "Clean weapon",** carried out **in Italy** in early 90s in conclusion What, turned out to be "bred up from transfer" 80 % Italian over- lytics, actually stoped action mother parties.

USA, Germany, UK, France and some other countries **An important role in the fight against corruption in** some states is given to taxes. **govoy management**.

For example, **U.S. law officials submitted a declaration of income and property of persons** spouses (spouse) and other over dependant members families.

one **from most corruptly independent known to indicate, to declare Canada's military service** . Canada attaches great importance to ethical values standards over to indicate, to declare service. HORSE How are you today? Contact, with point opinion degenerate- time, to indicate, to declare service in How are you today? country a most clean.

Legislation about to indicate, to declare service Canada includes a series of administrative bans on part-time employment in public service. However, the bans only concern these aspects of the business. Capacity to cause conflict of interest in government military service and **the State Code of Conduct adopted in 1985** provides an opportunity for certain categories of **officers** involvement of civil servants in certain types of work Telski activities parallel with to indicate, to declare service.

2.2. common opinion UN against corruption

The issue of corruption has been in the sight of the UN for more than two years. decades. This is precisely the understanding of the international character of the treaty. rupee, he is transnationality requirements acceptance spherical quantity over at the interstate level to neutralize the threat posed by ensures the security of the entire world community. Therefore, don't Tea is the focal point of the Global Programs implemented within the scope of UN programs in crime prevention and crime justice, There is a problem corruption.

The United Nations Global Program provides assistance to countries in the detection, prevention and suppression of corruption . According to the program, **The aim of any national program is** , first of all, **increase the risk and costs of corruption** ; second , **create** well **atmosphere indestructibility** , which? changed to want regulations games and to move-the location of its participants; third, to **ensure** final **compliance legality** . HORSE especially in frame programs under development mechanisms, contribution bigger transparency and reporting in fields to indicate, to declare nyh supply and International advertising transactions. Outside To go, for persons, from- responsible back development politicians for judges prosecutors workers Good- protector and monetary sizes organized studies.

one from **first International documents** in taken into account about-**It was adopted by the General Assembly on 15 December 1975** . **UN, resolution** , which, condemning "all kinds corruption", calls Right-evidence in frame to them National jurisdiction undertake all necessary measures to prevent crpin and punish offenders. further forward **over eighth Congress over warning crime and opposite nyu with criminals UN it happened accepted** special **solution**

" **Corruption in Public Administration** " , **Final guide** prepared by the SecretariatUN, « **practice quantity to fight with corruption** ", where stated next-blowing: as far as corruption between to indicate, to declare formal persons moon zhet flatten over Number potential competence all Species state- nyh programs, make it difficult development and to create threatening for individual personsand groups persons, in higher degree important, **with all states** :

1) **analyzed the adequacy of criminal legislation** , _ including procedural with norms Like this

Responding all types of corruption;

2) improved administrative and regulatory mechanisms for warnings corruption ;

3) **established procedures to detect, investigate and convict nia degenerate authorities** ;

4) developed legal provisions for confiscation of funds, and Real estate, Acquired in conclusion corruption ;

5) **took appropriate action against the businesses concerned natural with corruption.**

addition , corruption was one of the important **subjects of the special investigation . meetings Ninth UN Congress** (Cairo 1995).

In 1996 the UN General Assembly (UNGA) adopted a Resolution. lucia "to fight with corruption", which? calls with care race- Look at issues related to the international aspects of corruption, especially with regard to international economic activities, Done Corporate organizations.

Moreover known **declaration UN "HE to fight with corruption and bribe In International Business Transactions" 1996**, partner States which, among other things, undertake to recognize as states judicial a crime corrupt apps foreign to indicate, to declare formal persons and Cancel release from taxation quantities, over- radiant in format bribe from none special or to indicate, to declare companies

or physically faces Member State UN none public that- novice or face, selected in representative organ another countries.

Thus, the UN acknowledged the international nature of the problem. corruption and trying to find generally acceptable forms and methods of stopping it this case. All of the above documents are recommended important and does not really affect the resolution of the problem. Again These actions play an important role in shaping the norms of international law. and relevant to the subject under investigation and also capable of influencing norms of internal anti-corruption legislation and in general, spread Rights states international community.

2.3. common opinion Council Europe about judicial responsibility back corruption

In , **the Committee of Ministers of the Council of Europe adopted the Program . action over to fight with corruption _** in frame which? it happened supplied ad open to the signature of the **Criminal Law Convention . corruption** from 27 January **1999** .

Based on the main provisions of this international document to combat such crimes in the most effective way. The parties to the contract undertake to make appropriate changes. Amendments to domestic legal norms regulating : **rupee, judicial jurisdiction** over like this works; **responsibility legal entities** , sanctions and other measures of influence; **employee protection, justice** and witnesses **seeking; measures to encourage collection confiscation of evidence and proceeds ; specialization of organs and**anti-corruption **officials; to ensure cooperation protector sizes** within the country.

In the Preamble to the Criminal Law Convention against Corruption stresses that it should be done as a priority.general criminal policy aimed at protecting society from corruption including the adoption of relevant legislation and preventive measures quantity. It also talks about the threat posed by corruption. law enforcement, democracy, Right human, social justice, economic development, moral foundations.

The purpose of the Convention is to broaden, intensify and , as appropriate, the functioning of **international cooperation in the** ₤l. **Fishing Rights** participating countries contracts, with aim **prevention threats**

superiority live, democracy, Rights human, effective to indicate, to declaregift **management, equality and** social **justice principles curiosity, competition, economic development and** threatening

stability democratic institutions and moral fundamentals society. HORSE episode II

"Measures to be Taken at the National Level " **were determined kinds degenerate Crimes.** As such are:

— **active bribe** National **to indicate, to declare location any person (Art. 2nd);**

— **passive bribe** National **to indicate, to declare location any person (Art. 3);**

— **bribe members** National **to indicate, to declare assemblies (Art. 4);**

— **bribing foreign** public officials and members **new** foreign **government assemblies (Art. Art. 5, 6);**

— active and passive bribe in private sector (Art. Art. 7, eight);

— **bribe formal persons** International **organizations (Art. nine);**

— **bribe members** International

parliamentarian assemblies (Art. front);

— **bribe judges and formal persons** International **courts (Art. eleven).**

To separate article to ensure lots formulations degenerate front steps - use formal provisions in selfish purposes (Art. 12), laundering Income, received from degenerate Crimes (Art. frontend) and Crimes, related operations partner accounts (Art. fourteen).

However, the Convention does not prevent its implementation by the state.participant any criminal jurisdiction by virtue of with her National national legislation on other corruption compounds Crimes.

Analysis of the norms of criminal law established by the Convention (art. 2 - 11) Indicates that the contract extends the scope of legal entities corruption crimes.

With short stories European Rights to be attributed location contracts, on the liability of legal persons in connection with corruption Crimes. According to this Art. eighteen contracts **legal faces May to be bought justice on with the** criminal **investigative commission steps consisting of active**

bribery , zebnogo provisions in selfish purposes and laundering money _ qualificationtattoo in quality lots in fit with real common opinion and **partner accomplished in areas of interest none physically face, flow in** her

personal quality or in composition body legal face, which? forni- mom leader location in legal face _ by:

— fulfillment representative functions from name legal faces;

— application Rights over Adoption decisions from name legalsky faces;

— application control functions in frame legal faces;

— back participation lots physically faces in aforementioned judicial leniyah in quality crime partner (crime partner or provocative).

At the same time, most scientists are against crime. responsibility legal entities, other - back.

The very interesting question about this is, when the fact of political corruption is traced and parties computer scientists states or high school officers to indicate, to declare device.

In general , This maybe to indicate over customized character conceptual Research dovaniya or choice to them lighting in the media . What self over self- affirmsuniversal character corruption, in including and he is use as an instrument police authorities dishonest officers over various levels to manage. Legislation rowing countries, in especially Republic Kazakhstan, immortality provides judicial responsibility legal persons in Links with partner success degenerate Crimes, in difference from fight corruption

nyh legislation Republic Belarus and Russian Federation.

According to art. According to article 23 of the contract, banking secrecy is not an obstacle. implementation of measures to facilitate the collection of evidence; and skate Income from corruption.

Together with topics in fit partner Art. nineteen contracts "each one Side most-gets also legislative and other quantity, which? May is necessary for To go, with forgive myself live capture or otherwise path capture commissions and revenues from qualified crimesin quality lots in fit with real common thought, or Real estate, price to who is equivalent like this Income."

undertakes to take appropriate measures to protect witnesses , and other persons cooperating with justice in the fight against corruption, and also to support in International persecution persons, accused in Cor- cryptassisting each other in providing necessary information time, collection evidence confiscation Income, return criminals (Art. 22).

The Convention provides states with my general principles. international cooperation in the fight against corruption **- use of multilateral and bilateral international agreements trench** , in its absence , **obliges the parties to provide each other.** maximum possible **help** _ definite he is provisions.

article 27 contracts **determined order return people** _ **over-** committed **corruption crimes** lots in fit with this Agreement.

this **Agreement** because**corrupt persons**, such as after signing by states**no Crimes,** already **immortality May to use area** these **countries for avoidance judicial persecution** (as This dead also absencetwo sided deals about return between special countries).

Control over the application of the provisions of the Criminal Liability **Convention**Real estate **assigned** over **group states against corruption (GRECO).**

However, it should not be forgotten that **the fight against corruption** only only **alone** or substantially **quantity criminal lawvogo character, not effective** . On the contrary, it **can be It is dangerous** for society and states because it does not exclude it **completely** . **corruption** to indicate, to declare apparatus , **a only raises odds** back degenerate movements **partner side formal persons** .

What also immortality decides problems professional and moral Prepare Theneed to develop methods as well as training officers inclusive coup over minimization degenerate behaviour should- nostalgic persons apparatus to indicate, to declare to manage for all countries in Generally.

2.4. Civil Law Agreement responsibility back corruption

In 1996 the **Committee of Ministers of the Council of Europe adopted the Program** the **fight against corruption** and the **Civil Law Agreement open for signature responsibility for corruption** from 4 November **1999** .

HORSE contracts **undertaken attempt definitions corruption** (with Wow-Study: for the purposes of this Agreement).

Article 2 of the Convention qualifies corruption as **a necessity bribe, give or accept,** directly or indirectly, a **bribe** or **other bribeunnecessary advantage that deflects** proper performance **responsibilities buyer** bribe **or creates** unsuitable **advantages** .

The **purpose of the convention is to create effective legal instruments. general protection for persons harmed as a result of** acts of **corruption allowing them to protect their rights and** interests , including opportunity **taking compensation** back damage.

common opinion divided over **three sections** , which? encase: **measures** _ newly recognized , **international cooperation and executive control** , a also end provisions.

hour confirmation contracts **states acceptance** over myself **forced to take is principles and norms** in its domestic **legislation authority** with taking into account to them have National areas of interest and conditions.

HORSE contracts taken into account the following **questions** :

— **responsibility** (including responsibility states back actions corruption, loyalty public formal persons);

— **imprudence injured** : decrease compensation or refusal in Inside that Depending conditions;

— legal Force transactions ;

— **protection formal people** _ reporting about corruption;

— **sharpness and precision reports** and controls;

— taking proof ;

— **court decisions** on the protection of property necessary for the execution of the final decision and the continuation of the status quo Answers the topics covered;

— International cooperation .

Thus, **the Council of Europe has established** a **model** for harmonization . **legal norms, directed** as **against transnational** Like this **and** pro- What drives the creation of Good against **domestic corruption** favorable conditions for providing more effective legal interstate venous mutual aid in frame European geographical area.

2.5. Twenty principles Council Europe over to fight with corruption

corruption, over all stages human development is is seriousthreatening mother principles and values humanity. weakens belief citizens destroy the superiority and importance of finate in the rule of law, it violates human rights and hinders a successful society. World socio-economic development. HORSE Links with How are you today? Council Europe had accepted guiding 20 principles for to fight against corruption.

Twenty principles of the Council of Europefor to fight against corruption

1. **Take effective measures to prevent corruption and raise public** awareness and publicity **in this regard** ethic behaviour.

2. **Guarantee admission** National and International

corruption guilty .

3. **guarantee, What** them, **who Answers back** prevention, **researcher show, judicial chase and judicial decision over** cases **corruption, have independence** and autonomy, **relating to to them functions** , I'm in-lyayutsya Free from affect and have effective facilities, for To go What- collecting evidence by protecting those who assisted the authorities to fight with corruption and keep security investigations

4. **Provide** appropriate measures for **confiscation and confiscation** . **Answers Income** in

conclusion cases **corruption** _

5. **Provide** appropriate measures **to prevent pressure nia for lawyers**, deals with corruption cases.

6. **Limit immunity** from investigation and prosecution **judicial** decision in cases of **corruption or corruption** to the extent **necessary** walkable in democratic society.

7. **To support expertise** peoples or **bodies, responsible To combat corruption** and to provide them with the appropriate toolsand learning for execution their duties.

8. **financial** laws **and** authorities , **To be responsible for its implementation, to contribute to the fight against corruption to him in an efficient and coordinated manner** , especially in denial. Possibility of reducing taxes according to the relevant law or rule bribe or others expenses associated with corruption.

9. organization, operation and **acceptance Considered by public**

administrations when making decisions need to fight with corruption _ in features, **guarantee pro-transparency** _ Easy going with competence to fight.

10. **rights and obligations formal persons, to contain Requirements to fight with corruption** and **to ensurebye** relating to and **effective discipline precautions** ; to support greater specification of expected behavior from the publicnatural persons, relating to means (e.g, codes behaviour).

11. Ensuring that **appropriate audit procedures are developed** hunting with movements to indicate, to declare Services and public sectors .

12. **To approve role revision procedures in** preventionand **discovery corruption** outside Management organs.

13. guarantee, What system public responsibilitytakes into account the consequences of corrupt behavior public officers.

14. **Adopting transparent procedures** appropriate for the **public order embodies fair competition** and retention. to live corrupt officials.

15. **Encourage Adoption** selected representatives **codes behaviour** and to support regulations financing political parties and vote campaigns which? back off corruption.

16. **guarantee, What media have Right Free** receive **again- to give information over** problems **corruption** and exposed only topics og-wounds, which? has necessary in democratic society.

17. **Make sure civil law is taken into account obliges the fight against corruption, and in** particular effective facilities and Rights them, who's? areas of interest effects corruption.

18. Encourage Research over corruption _

19. **To be taken into account in the fight against corruption Attention all aspects possible he is Links with organized front footsteps** and

laundering Money.

20. **internationally** to the greatest possible extent **no cooperation** _ all regions **to fight with corruption** _

2.6. Activity International organizations over to fight with corruption

HORSE complicated legal fight corruption source of money over International level special importance have them, which? focused over securityglobal effectiveness of the fight against transnational corruption . Over earnings lots quality prevention and Suppression most dangerousfor individual states and International communities works, also which? had to want guaranteed International standards qualifications corruption crimes, unified jurisdiction parameters , disgust persecution and punishment criminals a also only-live pay back damage victims topics.

such international **legal instruments he is be interested** universal (single for all or majority to indicate, to declaregrants) as **well** as agreements **defining generally accepted standards** acceptance with to them local and two sided contracts.

Great role in **combining the** general approaches of **national approaches Legislatures of various states in the fight against corruption International organizations** systems UN, Recommendation Europe, World

bank, Organization of American States, Economic Organization pearl cooperation and development (OECD).

Eurasia in the fight against corruption Economic commission one economic Space (ECE It was established at the beginning of 2012 within the framework of CES). Republic of Belarus, Russian Federation and Republic of Kazakhstan one economic area.

Currently, the World Bank is of great importance. managed fight corruption politicians.

March **2007, the Board of Directors** unanimously **adopted it. strategy groups organizations World bank** , which?

directed overexpand the scale of assistance to client countries to developto indicate, to declare to manage and to fight with corruption. HORSE December **2007 of the year** it happened The **plan for the implementation of the strategy was published**, and **the CouncilDevelopment to indicate, to declare to manage and to fight with corruption** _

strategy valid **over four** most important **directions** : **support- ka** smooth **to manage and to fight with corruption** over country level, Reafgardstrengthening **corruption** in projects financed by the Bank **The role of the private sector in** efforts to improve governance and the fight against corruption in the public sector, as well as **support spherical efforts over interruption** scale **corruption** _

HORSE **2001 year** in composition World jar it happened created **Departmenton the fight against corruption, fraud and corporate companies decisions (INT)** in quality independent researcher sections.

Department **amount investigations** over accusations in cheatand and corruption in frame funded Bank projects, a also over apparent opinions in violations, Permitted employees institutions, and representative reports its opinions to the Bank management. In particular, regional leaders advance sections, Minister and Board over sanctions (If violated nia accepted legal and physically persons to cooperatewith the Bank) and Vice President of Human Resources (if violations have been committed)employees Jar) **for acceptance** further forward **precautions**.

hour need Department also **informs about Results they investigations authorities corresponding states**, in them cases, partner where in to go forward investigations found truths, which? May reference howl about Sound, What had violated laws given states.

World bank, to give important Attention problem corruption and based on his own research, **it should be considered. Corruption as a symptom of the fundamental problems of the state w"**, a immortality as basis or single factor, defining "diseases about-society." Also by creating a **global database that** exists in the world **management models, the World Bank** systematically **Perception of the extent of corruption and its contributions** poverty inequality and **low level economic development,** in Links with this developed **a key reform program** necessary **for** improvement formation **to indicate, to declare to manage** and **to fight with corruption _**

HORSE mine order and **common opinion over to fight with corruption organizations Economic Co-operation and Development** (OECD) important affect over opposition development corruption. HORSE frame analysis The provisions of OECD documents are quite complex .It was reviewed he is International legal Questions to fight with corruption.

Legal initiatives given organizations, in fields to fight with blind- rupee, **established,** mother path **over** two documents - revisedwith 1994 of the year « **Suggestions over to fight partner bribe in International nyh business operations"** from 23 May 1997 of the year and **"Contracts over fighting with bribing officials of fæġn government agencies to apply International business**

operations" from 21 November 1997 of the year.

I represent as an economic organization of developed countries. 70% of worldwide exports and 90% of foreign direct investment, OECD **gives Attention corruption** _ directly **related to the economy** , that is, it has only limited ambitions sphere, related creation in words "straight play ground" trade.

HORSE **contracts** over to fight with bribe formal persons foreign Go- government officials in international business transactions **taken into account phenomenon** _ in your name « **active corruption** » or "entities-bribery" in the terminology of national law and a crime, loyalty formal face, which? gets bribe.

This **Convention does not deal with private sector corruption. limited to individuals** and to active counter-**correction activities. rupee** formal **persons foreign states** .

take aim at contracts OECD a to create "functional old-alive." The Convention does not claim to be a substantial combination: participating States - Right independent vote quantity for entrance- nia legal sanctions, imposed back Shack bribe foreign to indicate, to declarenym formal persons a Results should to be comparable.

common opinion OECD **clarified concept "formal faces uig te "foreign enterprise"** global criteria The scale corresponding to the founding purpose of the OECD (item 4, item 1) lenia for unification of the state legislation.

Thus, each country has its own as a rule, **a public official will be understood as not merely a person appointed or elected** and bestowed In this context, legislative, executive or judicial powers powers, **but also** persons **performing** public duties, **regardless of** whether they are public officials or not. **harvest or hired special contract _**

Between International organizations **in to fight with corruption stands out Group states over to fight with corruption** (GRECO) (The English) **group related to states Against corruption, - GRECO) -** created **Council Europe in 1999** year.

Basis aim organizations a Help participating countries in the fight against corruption. GRECO sets anti-corruption standards (Requirements) with activities states and controls suitability to them application- tics. Group helps to find limitations in National fight corruption makes policy and recommends necessary legislative, institutional or operational measures. GRECO provides a forum for: Exchange of best solutions in detection and prevention rupee. Group formed from 49 states. Membership in GRECO immortality annoyedEurope however, in now time single immortality European to indicate, to declare vomit in composition groups has UNITED STATES OF AMERICA.

COURSE 3. CORRUPTION INVESTIGATION AND DIAGNOSIS AS BASIC, BASE, FUNDAMENTAL IMPROVEMENTS ANTI-CORRUPTION STRATEGIES.

INTERNATIONAL THEORETICAL AND PRACTICAL EXPERIENCE IMPROVEMENTS And PROMOTIONS

3.1. Experience development approaches with formulating fight corruption layer chattering International and National level.

3.2. Experience development and application strategies opposition corruption in stra- No East Europe and Asia.

3.3. Tasks Research and diagnosis corruption.

3.4. International instruments Research corruption.

3.5. National instruments Research corruption.

3.1. Experience in developing formulation approaches fight corruption strategies over International

and National level

transnationality of corruption in the present stage of history sky development all countries **requirements acceptance spherical quantity** over between-

people level for neutralization threats,

which? he is is isfor security of the whole world communities.

HORSE force How are you today? immortality only complicated however and, former Total, **Internationalno fight corruption strategy** in frame systems **legal, political sky, organizational mer** , directed over:

1) formation fight corruption mode society;

2) promotion awareness about damage corruption;

3) security International standards qualifications corruptiontwelve crimes merger jurisdiction parameters;

4) creation atmosphere transparency in first order, in monetary sphere for make sure opportunities describing degenerate works;

5) fit principle inevitability punishment;

6) security fair compensation damage from degenerate Crimes affected
To achieve these goals, almost every anti-

corruption organization. For example, The main **task of Transparency International** (hereinafter referred to as TI) is to **anti-corruption environment that excludes the possibility of its existenceformation and dissemination corruption _**

The most important aspect in the implementation of this idea **is** creation of **anti-corruption coalitions** accepting international actions against bribery, as well as implement their content by determining legal and moral criteria natural behavior. TI is actively **a horse-atmosphere of intolerance towards corruption, especially during an** annual nyh **problems Perception Index Corruption** (rice. 3.1.).

Rice. 3.1. directory perception corruption over data transparency International

back 2010 year by country Eastern Europe and Asia

Since any phenomenon is within the dynamics of an interconnected system, development, then any of the Indices is quite conditional; Indicates the width of the distribution of indicators. Wide enough replacement Borders often reflect the dynamics of change, not the real picture. denial, consisting of state points, including some types Wear where these materials are used frequently, including political technologies.

national anti-corruption strategy is to **reduce the** level of **corruption** in the Republic of Belarus **by eliminating the causes creators, the application of** adequate **law enforcement measures** ,as well as **through the creation of an intolerant attitude towards corruption in society. through the coordination of** various state forces and instruments buildings, public, International organizations.

HORSE process development relating to methodologies will be specified parameter ry quantitative and quality rating degree achievements specified targets.

Quantitatively, the level of corruption will be evaluated and monitored. Damage from corruption as a share of GDP, but qualitatively - through perception public and national experts at corruption levelsti with using National and international instruments and standards wrestle with corruption.

HORSE back then same time, also approach with evaluation over basis data International organizations level and National character corruption and degree Effect-activity opposition and to fight with he is should anytime think to identifytheir tolerant politicization on this issue. And so most aim data as competence accepted quantity over stand-stvuyu corruption, Like this and to fight with he is should think National data relating to buildings responsible back To collect and analysis necessary Mate- rials over given direction, and to them evaluation in flow format.

Tasks National strategies opposition and to fight with corruption:

1. To identify promising single, consistent and long-nuyu program to fight with corruption in frame which? will to apply-sya existing, operational importance of the program, having duties within its framework specific periods or stages of solving specific national problems nyh tasks, based over International standards.

2. Assign priority instructions

to fight with corruption.

3. To identify Events and resources for achievements prioritiesa also responsible structures and deadlines for their implementation.

4. To organise system tracing application fight corruptionnyh Events.

5. To create mechanisms Coordination fight corruption efforts Go- to Rice. 3.4. Approximate scheme of the element block "Measures of the executive power"anti-corruption strategy

3.2. Experience development and application strategies opposition corruption in East Europe and Asia

Eastern Europe and Central Asia at the beginning of the 21st century among the most corrupt regions in the world. especially high vein corruption continues countries CIS.

Many politicians openly admit that corruption is rampant (from Hellenic, en - "between, between", and demos - "people"; characteristic famous Me too- intensity or people) and continually report about her political will fight-with him. However, these claims are often not supported by specific individuals. movements. However Even when? Concrete quantity accepted, them rarely lead- dyat with urgent and concrete interruption corruption.

annihilation corruption - this is long term task. HORSE bill to fight against there is no single solution to corruption; anti-corruption measures should always be combined thief various incentives, including inhibitor and oppressive quantity.

By measurement application fight corruption programs various country- mi, important to determine interaction between yourself with taking into account her special that, What gives Results, a What - Number, and swap experience to fight.

fight corruption network for countries East Europe and Asia (hereinafter referred to as the AKC) is one of the regional programs of the Organization's Working Group. Organization for

Economic Co-operation

This program covers Albania, Armenia, Azerbaijan. can, Belarus, Bosnia and Herzegovina, Bulgaria, Croatia, Estonia, Georgia, Kazakhstan, Kyrgyzstan, Kosovo, Latvia, Lithuania, Ma- sedonia, Moldova, Montenegro, Romania, Russian Federation, Ser- to beat, Tajikistan, Turkmenistan, Ukraine and Uzbekistan.

OECD and EU countries are also involved in the work of ASC, International and public organizations.

main **purpose** is to support the member states of the organization. by creating a regional "platform" to discuss the problems of activities anti-corruption activities, information exchange Monitoring, identifying and disseminating and coordinating best practices activities providing Help countries.

3.3. Tasks Research and diagnosis corruption

For the development and implementation of anti-corruption technologies, deep and complex scientific research and analytical materials on all aspects of the manifestation of corruption, as historically Both in terms of space and in terms of space. They must extend from the system. Transparency International's (TI) dark data analysis is determined annually global ranking of the spread of corruption, criminology level logical study of normative and legal acts, analysis of ground acts authorities to systemic remediation in all forms and forms. legal relations, control of activities and continuing education of participants fire away given process.

Institute of Sociology of the National Academy of Sciences in 2005 Republic Belarus it was carried out big National to work over

How are you today? title. Over he is moment near 35 % citizens countries stated What corruption In Belarus - a common phenomenon. At the same time, about 15% of Belarusians he is ordinary phenomenon and almost my love How are you today? numbers pointed What collide-xia with he is. Later on local Research afflicted General prosecution ra Republic Belarus, in especially in Grodno fields. Results is-is-The following are: Less than 10% of survey respondents have nothing in their area. corruption, 18% see bribery as gratitude for a service, 42% schennyh know ok I'm waiting in bribery for problem solving.

The most dangerous thing is that the corruption in people's minds does not end. considered immoral. For the health degree of the society Also, to what extent a person who gives a bribe will be prosecuted in the society. Ku, as a result of this there is no hope of a solution to the problem and no gratitude for service and negative emotions (shame, resentment, humiliation) what etc.). Extreme danger in the interaction of society and state the state also lies in the fact that a bribe is not perceived in society. swear as mechanism social interaction.

About 3,000 corruption crimes are recorded annually. related with various forms corruption.

activity is carried outlife only over Unified basic knowledge, quantity coup which? has in fields various, however connected to each other spheres.

However, law enforcement has become more efficient To take action to detect and seize property of corrupt officials in order to compensation caused harm them.

If one Previously efforts preliminary investigations repaid immortality more 49.8 % caused corrupt officials damage, back then thanks to application-nyu Unified quantity recoverability reached 86.9 %. This contributingproductive work over to create Real estate corrupt officials in Sound including formalized over relatives and strangers persons. With creation Conclusion-Specialization of the Committee of the Republic of Belarus, its divisions and expansion interactions with others sections and Services effective ness given activities will in all bigger degree increase.

At the same time, the solution to the corruption problem not only in the field of law enforcement, but also The measures used in many areas depend on the interaction of the system. tei, and have wide range.

3.4. International instruments Research corruption

One of the consequences of the globalization of relations is: Corruption has become global. **The fight against corruption is not limited Establishing responsibility** for bribing officials . In mania, the phenomena that accompany bribery are taken: organized crime ness, laundering from money, received illegal by etc.

However, in recent years it has been adopted in various parts of the world. a little declarations and contracts directed over opposition blind- rupee as a global phenomenon. accepted contracts, norms Rights International character, compulsory for countries, approved ruyuschie these contracts. After a long preparation , **the Organization- time Unified Nations accepted common opinion against corruption** _

UN thinks What **to fight with corruption** This **task to indicate, to declare Gifts** and for he is productive yield necessary, inclusive and a cross-sectoral approach to corruption prevention calm down only to the measures criminal prosecution.

The Convention draws attention to the need for special arrangements. specialized to indicate, to declare sizes over to fight with corruption (stst. 6,36), to organize the selection of personnel for the state apparatus (Article 7) code of conduct for employees and other officials (Article 8) Ensuring transparency and competition in the implementation of public services supply and contracts (Art. nine), fascination civilian societies with to fight corruption, primarily through access to information about activities sti government agencies (Art. frontend).

The fight against corruption in the contract is connected with the implementation of measures. money laundering liability rupee (stst. fourteen, 24), hiding Real estate, clearly received Because ofdegenerate behave (Art. 25), obstacle justice in casesabout corruption (art. 25).

Convention, participating countries, not only criminalizes bribery of public officials (art. 15,16, 18), as well as embezzlement of state property (art. 17), abuse official position (art. 19), illegal enrichment (Art. 20).

It is recommended that it be recognized as criminally punishable. but also the promise or offer of some illegal advantage society, a also bribery extortion (art. fifteen, sixteen, eighteen).

States are calling for bribery of foreigners to be criminalized. strange public officials and international officials nyh public organizations (art. sixteen).

The UN also raises the issue of introducing the liability of legal persons. for corruption (art. 26). States are invited to enact laws Measures taken to protect witnesses and whistleblowers (art. 32, 33), to provide compensation for the damage suffered by individuals conclusion degenerate works (art. 35).

Moreover UN calls participating states International a commitment to active cooperation in the fight against corruption, including providing technical assistance in investigating facts about corruption; and rotation of financial resources obtained as a result of corruption operations in countries, which? they belong.

In 2000, the UN **ratified the United**

Nations Convention. tiv transnational organized crime .

transnational organized crime ness a important resource corruption in World. Behave requirements from member states criminalize corruption (article 8) and quantity for prevention and fight against it (art. nine).

Each of the participating countries, by acceding to this Convention, not only giving and receiving bribes, but also "both bid and offer" making persistent demands as well as bribing bribe in format any "illegal goods".

It is also new that the Convention prohibits bribery of foreign public officials.nh officials. The Convention proposes the use of the confiscated. Criminals have property to cover the costs associated with obtaining evidence . over situation. Participating countries contracts receive over myself compulsorystva handle friend friend Help in investigation named Crimes. If crimcannot be extradited to another country because of their nationality ,back then them should to be on trial in her country back works, loyalty over foreign whose territory is used in Convention norms against the interests of another country only in cases, where crime assigned over organized judicial groups, and a crime loyalty in frame transnational relationships.

A large-scale document was adopted by the American Organization.states in 1996 year. Inter-American common opinion against corruption already ra-durable 20 countries North and sunlight America.

It establishes responsibility, not just for active and passive. ny bribe, however and back other movements or inactivity formal persons,

aimed at obtaining illegal benefits as well as the use and concealment of corrupt property. document spreads Crimes commitment as within the country, Like this and in transnational relations.

"American Convention Against Corruption" wide understanding illegal corruption, which? immortality comes down with under- cup. Here includes: abuse of privacy information, state ownership by authorities, tries to seek any solution from public authorities for illegal situations. the purpose and misuse of any public property, money or security measures.

common opinion recommends participating countries set inhibitor quantity related Changes in formal, tax, banking Right.

role of international anti-corruption instruments, to fill and declarations, include political expressions and calls.

Thus, " **UN Declaration against Corruption and Bribery in International Law" domestic commercial trans relations** » calls to all countries of the world criminalizing foreign bribery, operates in the field of international trade relations. Release As in the example, they pay tax on money spent on bribes. many countries Peace, where tax paid with received reached.

It is known that close ties of corruption have formed in the process. election campaigns. Receives candidates for the selected post financial and administrative support from individuals and location, forced draw their debts.

In this context, **Resolution 24 (97)** states that mother of special rules that prevent corruption in law financing parties and choice campaigns (Principle fifteen).

Principle 6 of Resolution 24 (97) of the Committee of Ministers of the Council of Europe ropy demands that the immunity of the city's **top officials be limited** provide state investigation and prosecution perpetrators of corruption crimes to a level beyond omitted in democratic to indicate, to declare.

In 1996, the UN General Assembly local codes of conduct for public officials" . This Code It can be accepted as a model by all countries of the world. requires movement the loyalty of public officials and other officials to the public important (a immortality to indicate, to declare) areas of interest, call with productive

Work, cleaning impartiality and diligent relationship with community venous source of money. People office worker immortality should acceptance participation in bill in which? Personally interested (immortality confess conflict interests), in Sound number, after that care partner Services. HE IS Like this same requirements declarations Real estate provisions and received good, to reject from Gifts.

Following the UN, the **Council of Europe adopted a Model Code in 2000. for the behavior of public officials**. Optional wearinghowever, it is advisory in nature. This code covers a wider range More trouble than UN document. Pays more attention to blocking potential conflicts of interest of employees and a way out of difficulty situations (Articles 8, 13-16). Relevant regulations for a series countries, modern problems of party membership conflict harvest and his people responsibilities.

Active participation in corruption research and the development of tools opposition he is acceptance organizations, created also UN.

Like this **centre over warning International crime ; Office of Drug Control and Crime Prevention news Secretarial Unified Nations** jointly with **institute United Nations Interregional Crime and Research arrogance justice** advanced « **world program against blind- rupees** ." Aims to assist the participating States International relationships in to them efforts over to fight with corruption.

Within the framework of the World Program, Inter- international crime , **UN Anticorrosive Principles corruption policy"** and **"A set of anti-corruption tools"** , which? systematically recycled and is updated. Availablealready seventh version How are you today? document. named documents immortality have legal force and the advice of scientists for countries. on purpose to fight with corruption.

draft document " **Global Program Against Corruption** " corruption in economic, political and social nye, legal, administrative and cultural reasons. based Therefore, an effective struggle against it can only be based on interdisciplinary foundations. linear approach. The above documents **developed by the organization Presenting an integrated approach to states by the UN problem** by applying a series of interrelated measuresIt is political, organizational and legal in nature. These measures should be carried out over National, local and International

nominal level. Recommended set of anti-corruption tools: based on anti-corruption practices in different countries. Peace. The documents refer to the experiences of specific countries, nargile success in this area.

strategic **direction to fight with corruption a participation of civil society** in this struggle . Obviously, just It is possible to achieve effective results with its most active participation. Results fight against corruption Generally.

key **connection societies in to fight with corruption has** and independent, free **media** . They were phoned we awaken society, raise the spirit of intolerance towards corruption and natural persons, politicians convicted of corruption, to identify the individual truths corruption and to add to them promotion.

In order for journalists to fulfill these functions, extensive knowledge of the activities of the state apparatus. in developed countriesno, special laws enacted compelling public officials poidejournalists and citizens with all the information they need, except those that are not subject to free distribution by law . organ- reduction UN impulse states

Cancel censor make facilities mass- howl information financially independent from to indicate, to declare organs.

The construction sector ranks second in the anti-corruption strategy. authority to indicate, to declare institutions, ingenious lead productive to fight with corruption.

Difficulties has in Sound, What give account lead How are you today? to fight "in have-venous house", leaning over over them peoples, which? May to be themselves far immortality without-sinner. As a result, UN organizations recommend its widespread use. separation of powers mechanism using the same bodies to fight corruption in others bodies, by jumping obstacles circular bail and Stationary secrets.

Independent courts should have capability endure

unbiased **Answers over works about corruption** in sizes authorities.

The legislature, as an independent body of government, adopt regulations that limit corruption and control VAT work executive organs.

HORSE especially in documents highlights importance creation independent parliamentary commissions to investigate the highest corruption cases now formal persons. Inside executive sizes offered allocating independent structures that exercise control over activitiesto indicate, to declare employees and disclosure truths corruption.

examined , UN organizations,all work to indicate, to declare mechanism over principles transparency lowerparity society responsibility former he is, over basis sovereignty Rights.

The documents of UN agencies emphasize that it should be emphasized. on warning, not punitive measures against corrupt officials denial of corruption. Based on this, it is necessary, first of all, to develop. not criminal but state and administrative law. norms the last two branches of law provide the proper working order to indicate, to declare sizes and their employees.

UN Global Program Against Corruption invites Statesto create special countrywide organ over investigation mostserious truths corruption. HE IS should occur from most

Experienced ra- police officers, investigators, tax professionals, finance and customs works. UN also offers mine model project law for this body. Systematic control of officers proposed to be done with special external and internal assistance buildings in executive sizes authorities.

UN offers everybody countries to accept **codes behaviour** employees, which? it contains to want as **regulator,** Like this **and law enforcement What-We.** Therefore, it is necessary to check the correctness of filling out the declaration yourself. organizations should carried out external Management bodies.

World application to go over path vote employee, to them learning and to support zheniya over service immortality Leader sections, a special employee Agency. What contributes to the suppression of formation in the state ? bodies of informal groups (relatives, clans of immigrants from somewhere, comrades at old work, etc.). Otherwise situation This encourages development systemic corruption and creation in sizes authorities organized judicial groups managers.

Great importance is attached to these UN documents. the role of audit conducted by independent accounting chambers and alny inspection bodies. Auditors are offered It is necessary to expose all financial and economic activities of the state. necessary and municipality organizations, institutions and businesses.

3.5. National instruments Research corruption

Mother tools Research corruption in Republic To be- larus are: strategic countrywide programs; complicated

no programs Research; local and local programs; analyticalscientific work of state bodies; monographic works; enketirovanie (selective and continually); surveys citizens (written and mouth-no); Public relations; performances in groups; development trainer programs and inclusion in system learning in universities Republic To be- larus trainer disciplines "Corruption and he is public danger".

HORSE especially one from National tools Research corruption is most accurately a written citizen survey new research method. In 2011, a survey was conducted among citizens. From Republic Belarus. Between suggested estimated respondents There were also problems with the issue of corruption. Finished- no answers given over rice. 3.5.

Rice. 3.5. Results questionnaire by citizens problem corruption (2011 G.)

survey, most Survey respondents were particularly concerned about corruption and bribery. Felt by people aged 30-59 with higher education, service and trade providers, entrepreneurs. Pain- Residents of regional centers are less aware of corruption. For this problem, companies actively pay attention to entrepreneurs, workers in the industry service and trade. Lawsuits were filed against the courts, military concerns about the stratification of society. Proportional-with quota Noah sampling it was with survey one and a half thousands (1500) respondents.

COURSE 4. CORRUPTION AND THE LAW STATE: LEGAL BASIC KNOWLEDGE ANTI-

CORRUPTION STRATEGIES

4.1. role institutions Rights in opposition corruption.

4.2. courts and corruption.

4.3. law enforcement sizes and corruption.

4.4. political corruption and roads opposition he is.

4.5. problems opposition political corruption.

4.6. Sort Management corruption.

4.7. Corruption and citizens. Corruption and business.

4.8. roads opposition Management corruption.

4.1. role institutions Rights in opposition corruption

Civil society is a **set of** horizontal **relations.I am waiting citizens providing application to them amateur performances and h-economic**, social, socio-cultural, politicaltic and other **fields vital activity** in selected to them forms.

The foundation of civil society is that of citizens and their communities. states in vote priorities preferences and forms activities and electoral responsibility, the consequences before the state. warranties such freedom.

Civilian freedom Done topics fuller How more mom- forehead, intellectual and socio-cultural basis for self organization citizens.

The most important feature of the rule of law is self-government. limitation. Fundamentals of legal civil society stva has assumptions "immortality citizens society, a society citizens";

"immortality have obeys general good, a general good follows from

Real Estate"; "It is the citizens, not the state, that give freedom to the citizens. measure of freedom to the state"; "It is not the laws that underlie human rights, but

WA human - in basis laws."

It is one of the regulation systems of social relations. In modern society, an orientation towards the construction of legal regulations, The state where choices are first seen in the fight against corruption belong to legal toolkit.

a much **broader concept than "legislation"** . Law is also legal customs and traditions and mechanisms for their enforcement. norms Rights (procedural Right, former Total), and legal ideology and etc.Examining the role of law in the fight against corruption, limited to free or critical comments on the package normative legal actions about opposition corruption. Necessary sufficient level all the rest components concepts "Right".

chef **factor opposition degenerate norms** rights **are publicity** . But the state has opportunities. to prevent the adoption of such rules of law. The decisive role here can play a legal anti-corruption expertise of bills rebel developments and discussion.

Anti-corruption expertise is a complex of mine. activities to determine the rules of law that can create such a framework relationships between topics that increase probability to them entrance degenerate relationships.

Tall level corruption objectively requirements from states carrying out a mandatory anti-corruption expertise, being one of the constituent features of the legislative process along with the legal process wild and language expertise.

Power, which opens its activities, becomes transparent and therefore effectively controlled by society, achieving institutional transformations education, combating corrupt legislation, vue purge corruption reasons.

eliminating corruption as a public relations system **The state can** only **engage in joint activities with the structures . tours and** NGOs . without the public control over the activities of public authorities and authorities local government, self-development and continuous improvement pearl civilian societies earning corruption impossible.

4.2. courts and corruption

The court should be an institution that is not under guardianship and protection. any power to occupy a suprapolitical position in society. her the activities of the court should be guided only by the Constitution and norms mom Current legislation.

It is important for legislators to free the court from material need, and stvo - from the possibility of observing it. Ownership of ships and judges, especially residence and appointment to office should to create opportunity or address for Thanks.

It is unacceptable to exist in countries that have undertaken a difficult task. anti-corruption activities, manifestations of mediating facts Services, discredit as self justice, Like this and system in Generally.

complaints over activity courts and judges limitations in system front body investigations Crimes, conditioned factor transition period, often have reasonable character. July immortality little, application task-chi over creation in Republic Belarus academies justice and excellence- Monitoring the activities of the established Investigative Committee of the Republic of Belaruswill to support formation as expired employee composition destiny- Noah systems, Like this and conditions for high school level fulfillment he is tasks.

Corruption schemes in the judicial systems of various countries are difficult to detect. since the litigation, it can be proved in terms of the injured partyby law - hostile and does not prove the illegality of the decisionThe fact of corruption is, however, only an indirect confirmation. This The party does not have the procedural right to obtain control because this is the responsibility of the relevant law enforcement authorities. At the same time, theirin a position to maintain local leadership normal relationships with courts purposes Answers their duties.

Some countries not only deny the existence of judicial corruption systems, however and missing programs counter reaction.

HORSE necessary cases important to create conditions reference Flat publications from court room, What will exclude violations and to support formation more high school public picture judicial systems,It is against the established perception tradition of the closedness of the judicial system. HORSE countries with advanced legal system (in UNITED STATES OF AMERICA, Britain) open- toast judicial meetings higher judicial examples guaranteed immortality only legislation, however and Done over application. For example, in United States of America meetings Sublime court to be to see over TV - session, meeting, session

Denmark broadcasts to the whole world and meets the work of the court in the mod anyone can do this in real time. Also for translation meetings to indicate, to declare channels.

Transparency in the evaluation of cases that "resonate" in the highest judicial institutions Stations allow society to control the judiciary, not allow it. laya affect over he is topics or otherwise path and handle abuse _

important that it is **formed in the judiciary of states** . a community **whose activities will be based on the principle of no addictions judicial power _**

Another way to fight corruption in the judiciary is states Centre Europe a Update judicial composition.

In general, the constitutional **image** of the court largely **depends on the behavior of the court. judges**, to them sincere, devoted passion justice.

Constitutional law gains strength in beliefs and values.driven by a particular type of activity that society values highly, and when you're ready to hear it. In a constitutional society, it is strictly determined by fate.yami, practically concretization belief in TRUE Right and her high school goals, constitution, and topics most make somebody right her high school meeting.

hour declaration independence violated principle systems checks and balances of state organs and loss of quality of the judiciary stvo. **to reduce corruption** judicial systems **probably by the judiciary as** an independent institution . **pearl provisions** in society.

4.3. law enforcement sizes and corruption

In the legal field of civil society under construction, law enforcement organizations directly carry out the fight against corruption. However features development societies in conditions transition period and created vanilla socially directed Market economy immortality can immortality reflectover to them activities. Economic and social crises, Changes in systemsocial, interpersonal and family relations, stratification issues society, high school dynamics legislative Changes reflective necessary kilometer Answers problems inclusive character, created for law enforcementthread spheres complicated conditions fulfillment they tasks.

The effectiveness of the law enforcement system is affected by: girl factors shift generations and level education experts.

experts often note growth inefficiency work law enforcement thread bodies, What creates problems relationships between communityvomit and to indicate, to declare. People recommendation also law enforcement sizes for reference civilian control, have advice completelyurine does not always provide the appropriate level of solution that occurs. problems in basis which? - availability manifestations corruption over background under-tatkov in vote, growing, providing and employee politics. HORSE back then same timeMe too, it is forbidden confess decrease rollers dialogue between civilian to organizetion and citizens with law enforcement authorities in sphere anti-wiya corruption, exclude possibility formation visibility interaction action between society and to indicate, to declare also real her absence.

At the same time, the main body of state power, controlling and coordinating law enforcement activities, including including the fight against corruption, the prosecution is responsible. compliance with the law, protection of human rights and freedoms. This is reflected as at the level of public dialogue in the form of various activities, creation of its activities through the media and design and legislative activities.

The image of the state is reflected in the face of law enforcement officers, which serves the interests of the people. Thus, preparation and activities activities of employees in this field, absolute certainty Request reflects corporate interests . In this case, the state is reduced to just a common cause for employees, instead of res publica, the affairs of the people. In this process, it is necessary to return what was lost. today concept "formal debt."

image of an employee who doesn't fit in

their pre- task **Its purpose is to destroy the image of the state in** the eyes of the citizens and democracy, separation of powers, contradictions with the rule of law, Rights and individual liberties.

An important factor in solving anti-corruption problems is tḧẹ̃reforming law enforcement . But at the same time necessary complicated Changes from legislative level former stimulant anti-corruption behavior by introducing the protection agency Right victims from corruption. hour How are you today? important location in system quantity fight corruption legislation a decision about protection, as collaborators nicknames law enforcement systems, Like this and representatives all other sizes authorities, declaration about to be to them famous truths corruption in to go forward Work.

4.4. political corruption and roads opposition he is

Term **"political corruption"** , over first seeing, like that unkor- rectal, as far as actually degenerate works contacted only partner official abuses of authorities. officer concept person in legal science is associated with its presence in the executive arsenal. administrative powers based on power activitiessti as lesson To go or other kind activities in frame providedhe is Right and forces. With politics given concept immortality related.

political corruption , is is yourself apical medicine corruption _ lots to separate- from the base level (Fig. 4.1). The truth is selfish motives downstream levels social organizations (authorities less than ranks, teachers, doctors, etc.) has a concrete arrangement of material: Clearly stipulated quantities from money or units requested Services.

Rice. 4.1. Sort corruption by levels degeerate Crimes

hour political corruption and dimension fee, and myself her

truth often **hidden** from eyelash public and law enforcement structure

kind. HE IS there truth harmfulness lots phenomenon for Special human immortality lots- visible. Exactly How are you today? character contributing separation point opinion Research- voters political corruption. paradox is is in Sound, What definitely devastating with point opinion live, phenomenon in eyes theorists political sky to manage rotary in original detail managerial in-itmetinwhose abrasive nature is sometimes questioned. heresy apical corruption connected with basis offsets in system "aim - facilities". Regulator basis to indicate, to declarebut legal relationships implies open correlation source of money poly- tic Administration with her strategic and tactics what-lyami corrosiveness in How are you today? process visible in Sound, What also to use- call regulator still source of money topics sovereignty over- start persecuted not implied live targets. HOWEVER at that time, What This definitely deflection, a immortality "correction delivered tasks in fit with necessity moment", speaks he is truth, What covered under corner- Grey democratic slogans targets also attentive thought I'm in-

lyayutsya selfish and discredit self idea democracy.

In summary, **political corruption** is defined as *behavior . deviating from the official duties of a public office underby the action of private material or status goals or violations regulations, forbidding definite* *kinds special affect.*

In fact, political corruption officially entitled to a certain "error" Decision making process. This "error" is associated with these benefits. joyful, which? legally has in arsenal political lessonand act as a covert or open temptation. Therefore, the spread interpreting political corruption as "acts committed" made to provide some incompatible advantages with formal tasks formal face, which? illegaland uses it to illegally remove his position or status. any benefit to himself or any other person for purposes contrary to wrong tasks and rights other people."

the **subject's desire to increase their power potential , without being obvious** at first Look, **financial gain.** However, having power within yourselfstu as political and administrative source potentially a sufficient incentive and motivation to deviate from non-corrupt behavior pearl performance of the subject's functions sovereignty.

HORSE as a result, pervert understanding have political WHO- opportunities and tasks political figure leads to with neglect Public Interests. Political corruption violates the act responsibility for the public or civil system order and, from here, devastating for them systems.

Because the public interest is higher for social systems private , then violations for personal gain no yourself Behave political corruption _

Again in given situations difficult to make a decision, who must stand over protection public areas of interest and to be their guarantor.

Guarantee here get dressed couple character: with one hand, in quality-one of them must be the head of the officially appointed state. a wife is such a duty; but on the other hand, it acts as the guarantor. and say if-as a counterbalance to various situations to indicate, to declare public organizations, activities everybody individual.

The problem of political corruption has results. As a result of corrupt political agreements, capture of raw material bases and habitat, including foundations release wars.

4.5. problems opposition political corruption

The penalty for bribery was provided by the Ham-laws. Murapi (4 thousand years ago) was founded by Egyptian pharaohs. father The harmful effect of this antisocial phenomenon is felt in any country. immortality, whatever happens from to indicate, to declare devices or traditions.

sharp increase in corruption was noted during the formation of the market relationships in XIX century. Simultaneous seen and first trials anti- actions at the legislative level. However, a significant change in anticorrosivecorruption situations none in World, none in individual states immortality dead.

Only **in second my love XX century** _ when? **to fight with corruption** in a little countries **it happened planted in rank to indicate, to declare politics** _ successful former-to beat minimization he is affect over all spheres vital activity society.

HORSE How are you today? relationship is is interest experience them states, which? have most countless managerial apparatus. This, former Total, UNITED STATES OF AMERICA, Germany, United Kingdom, France, Chinese and rowing others countries.

In the United States, anti-corruption laws are characterized as: emergency hardness _ Like this, back various kinds corruption - bribe,

recoil (pay parts illegal from money party of the transaction) and others - three times the fine for bribery or jail time From 15 years or simultaneously and in aggravating conditions Charter - deprivation freedom term up to the age of 20.

Legislation United States of America provides punishment back Shack and taking fee back Services, incoming in a circle responsibilities formal faces. promotions, over American live, formal maybe receive only office-socially - from state. punishment back breach How are you today? norms - good or deprivation freedom former 2nd years or integrity penalties.

On the basis of transactions between

any person **about entering the** civil service . yes, guilty claim or receipt of money or property benefits nie to assist in entering public service. Guilty shall be punished with imprisonment of up to one year or a judicial fine of up to three years. the amount received or received, or a combination of both types of penalties. Exceptional is is activity special agencies over hire owner permission Join in Set over to indicate, to declare service.

fight corruption legislation United States of America wears systemic character . It also consists of **legal regulations that regulate it. lobbying, banking, exchange and other activities** . and ho- While this is not a guarantee of complete eradication of corruption, in the United States level much lower, How in other states.

to fight with corruption relax topics What **in United States of America** actually **Number to them-municipalities for civil servants** . **Any official,** including the President , congressmen and senators, **maybe to be attractive with** judicial **responsible**, _ Although and in special OK, after that suspension her from positions.

Another **important area of anti-corruption strategy** United States of America **a prevention corruption** in system to indicate, to declare service to want. It is based on the **introduction of the** so-called **"administrative"** .morality " representative yourself ethic and discipline norms.

The Government **Services Code of Ethics was first adopted in** the USA . **In 1958** , each former **face, found over state service, must** :

— raising adherence to moral principles and the state devotion persons parties or public authorities;

— role play constitution, laws UNITED STATES OF AMERICA, decrees sizes authorities and never immortality support them, who runs away from to them yield;

— work full time for a fixed fee necessary efforts and thoughts for fulfillment they responsibilities;

— find and implement the most effective and cost-effective ways stove solving tasks;

— never discriminate by giving to anyone paid or unpaid special benefits or privileges, Do not accept benefits or gifts for yourself or your family under the circumstances. Wow, which? May to be interpreted as coup over yield formal responsibilities;

— not making any promises regarding official duties because a civil servant cannot act privately stnoe face in execution to indicate, to declare positions;

— immortality to join none Flat, none Relatively in advertising relationshipswith the government if This conflicting conscientious to apply formal responsibilities;

— never immortality to use hidden and formal in- formation for personal gain;

— open cases corruption also to them identification;

— follow these principles conscious What state duty ness is an expression public trust.

code, Although and had advice character, in further forward it happened OS- New legislation on the "management ethics" of US civil servants .Outside Also, limited Right to indicate, to declare worker over side (over part time) earning, dimension to who immortality should

exceed fifteen % wage over positions.

This restriction applies to the officials of all branches. authorities, back exceptional members Senate UNITED STATES OF AMERICA. officers, appointed President UNITED STATES OF AMERICA, generally immortality May receive which? to want back then none it was Incomeservice life for services and activities beyond frame direct service responsibilities.

ex-officers , their limitation business activities valid in flow two years after that exit in resignation.To them forbidden fulfill representative functions also solution establishment we executive authorities Concrete works, which? processed with managedHow are you today? to indicate, to declare worker in flow of the year, pre-perfect schenie her Services. biennial ban spreads and over former "stale- shih officers" executive authorities. These immortality should support con-so you with former Location Work, immortality May to introduce anyone's areas of interest over

anyone question former topics Section, in which? them service or a little or public employees How are you today? departments.

Another important provision of the **anti-corruption strategy US governments** are **the same for** all branches of **government rules restricting the receipt of gifts by an official** from individuals and organizations.

Therefore, a U.S. senator and members of his staff, Accepting gifts from natural and legal persons who can May be interested in having the Senate pass certain laws The total value of the gifts during the calendar year is the new More than $100. The value of gifts one senator receives from another senator other sources (except relatives) during the calendar year, total should exceed $300. The Code of Ethics, gift payment allowances to individuals in the form of travel. Senate new limit of three days (and two nights) and seven nights for domestic travel days (and six nights) for trips abroad. These distribution restrictions vagabond also and over members senator families

Member rooms representatives Congress United States of America owner Right receive over-dark colors in flow calendar of the year general cost immortality more 250 dollar.

This restriction also applies to the employees of his office. hour How are you today? everybody to present, including Gifts spouses formal persons, Market Toswhosprice exceeds $100 must be declared. These restrictions spread over all Gifts, Moreover Gifts from relatives.

For other officer categories wail limitations over taking Gifts. to indicate, to declare office worker and her spouse (husband) may accept a gift within one calendar year. whose total price does not exceed $100. to have a gift above the allowable value, officer, girl 60 days to go past her in corresponding his organ departments.

As the analysis shows, the United States is a highly effective system, create conditions for productive to fight with corruption.

basis of criminal law on bribery in the **UK** and (corruption) to create **Live about bribe in public to organizetion 1889 g. and laws about warning corruption 1906 and 1916 Good game.**

The first of these laws condemns the request for bribery or bribery.a gift, loan, tip, or anything else that has value as a means of motivating an employee make anything or abstain from fulfillment anything.

The person found guilty of such an act, imprisonment or payment of the value of a gift, loan or prize the award he received. Also, it loses the right to be. scolded or assigned to any a term of public service for seven years. In the event of a second conviction, the perpetrator may be punished. may be permanently deprived of official rights, any compensation or pensionhonour formal.

In a separate corpus delicti of the crime of corruption, English lawrequest highlights bribe with aim taking honorary awards . most- responsibility for both givers and recipients bribe. bribe giver punished deprivation freedom over term former two years or (and) good over discretionary power court. venal - deprivation freedom former from 3 months and/or legal maximum penalty (**Law about warning abuse with award-winning 1925 g** .).

live about sales shipments 1809 g. in prints live about corners-Law No. 1967 is **liability against corruption.** sales, purchases, transactions with aim **taking** none **positions** , in Sound including and work over for rent as in in Unified kingdoms, Like this and under British rule. Perpetrators are punished with imprisonment for a period of time. former 2nd years and deprivation Rights forever, forever, always occupy relating to location.

English law is considered independent body Crimes bribe judges and judicial officers. faces, cat- Rye offer or to give judicial formal none present or monetary fee with aim affect over her formal behaviour or action, and the judge who accepts the award commits a crime what, punishable good or deprivation freedom former 2nd years.

the UK 's anti-corruption strategy, **a program is also being launched to promote** the principles of truth- **honesty** and integrity .**in all fields life** society, in

Sound including over to indicate, to declare service.

HORSE October **1994 g.** it happened **created** independent advice **Committee over standards (behaviour)** in public (to indicate, to declare) life. HORSE partner being Board entry front official public numbers, in Sound includingtwo member parliament. HORSE tasks Board includes: study and level norms over-behindheads of all public institutions, including all actswia, related with to them monetary and advertising activities; producing "recommendations to improve the moral criteria of public participants"life." With to them number had assigned all ministers, to indicate, to declare employees,members National and European parliaments, higher officers all non-governmental organizations, representatives of local governments. At the same time, **special consideration of the Committee is not recommended. cases violations standards** behaviour, a focus over format-research institutes general principles venerable participation in public life.

HORSE **1995 g. Committee formulated Seven principles to indicate, to declare venous work** officers - some kind of code behaviours:

— only in the public interest, actions to obtain material and financial benefits for themselves, her families and friends;

— corruption - any financial or other dependency on external persons or organizations that may influence yield formal debt;

— objectivity - unbiased decision all Questions;

— accountability - responsibility back accepted movements former general stvom and providing complete information in situation public controls;

— openness - maximum informing of society about everything decisions and actions, their validity (as well as reduction of knowledge null also need fit higher public interests);

— honesty - mandatory disclosure of one's private interests, taking all measures related to public duties Answers possible conflicts in use public areas of interest;

— leadership - commitment to leadership principles and personal examplein standards public life.

Despite themselves over yourself violations data standards immortality cause back yourself That-failures results and taken into account only as breach "Code chessti", them played role deterrent factor a in to fight with corruption.

fight corruption legislation France sent over to fight with formal Crimes to indicate, to declare officers as well as making political and administrative decisions. The impact of the activities of political parties using illegal methods today financing and hold election campaigns.

The first direction **was as early as 1919, when Ugo- had a code of conduct activated an article banning the state Any official working in the company for 5 years after resignation** , those they control while in public service. what business completion How are you today? Requirements punished deprivation freedom former two years and good in size 200 thousand franc.

In 1946, then **in 1992**, in connection with **the adoption of the State Charter venous service, responsibility** over given article **it happened bored**.

And all same French legislation gives more Caution executive nistrative a immortality judicial quantity punishment. hour How are you today? persecuted head- no aim - prevention unsuitable Links personal monetary between recess and yield formal functions to indicate, to declare worker.

French legislators are less harsh than Americans. that- Newcomers are not required to file an income statement, and examination over professional activity after that layoffs formalwith public service less controlled definitely.

strangeness French fight corruption legislator- stva, where **government** officials can **join you- forests without losing their status**. They are allowed to combine their studies boots with optional location over local level. If one same them selectedto the national parliament, they then have to leave the service, but The right to return to the former office after the expiration of the parliamentary powers position without any restrictions. In France, legal basic and organizational principles for the promotion of income and property declarations steve high-ranking workers to indicate, to declare device.

Until the middle of the 19th century, corruption **in Sweden was only** Good. One of the results of the modernization of the country was a set of targeted measures. It aims to abolish mercantilism. Since then, state regulation rationing involved more households than firms and was established however over incentives (by taxes, privileges and subsidies), not including over prohibitsand permissions. Opened **access** to internal government interventions . **documents** and established an independent and **effective justice system** . At the same time, the Swedish parliament and government , They began to seek **ethical standards for managers and their uses.** completion. Just a few years later, honesty has become the social norm. among officials. At the beginning of the modernization of the state wage system fees high-ranking officers exceeded earnings workers12 to

15 times, but over time this difference has decreased to two. multiple. Today **Sweden has one of the lowest rates. rupee** in World.

These examples of the fight against corruption, Examples of ways to combat it for states wishing to put it into commercial use floor fight corruption legislative and advice quantity.

4.6. Sort Management corruption

Everyday corruption is generated by the interaction of ordinary citizens given and officials. It includes various gifts from citizens and services. official and members of his family. This category also includes: nepotism (nepotism).

Business corruption occurs when government and business interact h. For example, in the event of a labor dispute, the parties enlist support judges with aim statement Answers in mine use.

Corruption sublime authorities valid with political guide-dstvo and sublime courts in democratic systems. HE IS concerns on foot-shchih also authorities groups, dishonest behaviour which? formed in wasp-politics in ways that harm their own interests and the interests of the electorate.Over figure 4.2 highlighted all kinds corruption in addictions from To go,

who abuses formal forces. allocation kinds corruptionin addictions from To go, who a bribe giver (rice. 4.3), over degree again- regularity degenerate Links (rice. 4.4). schema Species corruption in adhere to- value from spheres and levels degenerate

Rice. 4.6. Sort corruption in addictions from spheresand corruption levels Links

4.7. Corruption and citizens. Corruption and business

In everyday life, society is more often faced with its manifestation. corruption in the administrative system at the local, household level strative relationships, Education and health care.

units, **latitude and manifold public relationships to identifyLie importance participation civilian societies in prevention blind-rupee** lots higher, How to fight with corruption only themselves employees.

The reality of the development of society is such that it is not the fight against corruption. necessarily conditioned by the attainment of a democratic society level. va. It can also be authoritarian under anti-corruption slogans. management models that provide a certain level of countermeasure action given phenomenon.

optimal basis for the formation of conditions **fight corruption** in order to meet the interests society is **right in the process of interaction with the state** . sound **civilian society** _ built over principles of democracy.

But the main condition for the development of democracy is necessary - transparency of mechanisms for the achievement of rights and accessibility for citizens; and baud, given to man with moment birth.

Demonstrating successful anti-corruption experience in foreign countries In the fight against corruption, only Decisions due to various conditions for the formation and development of states. Thus, there are numerous options for each of the countries. vote fight corruption quantity.

For example, **with the convergence of interstate relations, Issues of ratification of international normative conventions need to be resolved.** Also of the UN and the Council of Europe **to combat corruption** . Which to ensure Entrance concepts illegal enrichment. The **concept of** illegal enrichment applied , **a search for corruption** . In this case to condemnIt is not necessary to prove that he is a potential corrupt official. chal bribe. HORSE definite conditions sufficient prove, What the property and assets of this official cannot be explained by legal sources of income.beat. This is in a sense a limitation of the presumption of innocence, however, Considering the extreme danger of such a public evil as corruption, many democratic states gone over similar limitations.

Estonia is one of the countries whose economies are in transition. which has been most successful in reducing corruption. where one of the most important elements of the success achieved in this country, **application**

systems "electronic governments".

Electronic procedures, personal interaction citizens **partner employees**. Potential bribe giver He doesn't know exactly who he should be addressing.pour a bribe. Similarly, taking a bribe is difficult because any attempting to establish personal contact with the customer, bypassing electronic shopping knowledge automatically raises doubts about the good the publicity of the officer's intentions and tiv with appropriate sanctions

it **is due to circumstances. inefficient and confusing procedures for** dissolving and processing them or other permissive movements. Often existence of many stations and queues while solving some problems event degenerate relationships.

HORSE World available countries, where formal, also developing them or other norms or Charter arrangement, absolute prove public authoritiesand public need and Benefit suggested to them quantity and process-Stupid If one is he immortality smoke prove to them Benefit, them taken into account unnecessary. Mexico has a " deregulation ombudsman". whose recipient has the right to suspend normative acts , destroy Rights citizens or provocative corruption.

Negative impact on the development of economies and living standards of countries citizens render corruption in budget sphere. This characteristically immortality only for countries with youth democratic Date, however and for countries

"Old" Europe, USA, Canada and Australia. **lobbying interests** inclusion in the budget of expenses for certain **industries and their financing** arrogance **a** typical **example** manifestations **degenerate schemes.**

There is always a frontal attack attempt against corruption . over serious political conflicts HORSE International experience there Quite a few examples when? ambitious and large scale trials to fight with corruption brought with lots modest Results, as For example, in Lithuania, What call-shaft frustration in society and caused with political crises.

Large expenditures on anti-corruption measures, including creation specialized buildings over to fight with corruption immortality anytime

led to a significant improvement in the situation and aroused skepticism relatively hopes he is overcome

radicalism to fight with corruption determined immortality 1 not only with the presence and absence of **political will , but also with the ratio.** political **resources** and tremendous **resistance** faces anti-corruption activities.

Obviously, the process of overcoming corruption in the Republic of Belarus Russia will be long-term, as in other countries. To move instead of improving the anti-corruption policy. you will have to do it gradually, step by step, as everything accumulates successfully. experience and application possibilities.

However, statements that corruption is an "incurable" phenomenon, erroneous, because historical **examples show the truth. the possibility of overcoming corruption through** consistent, permanent means vogo **application systemic actions** to combat corruption .

Most pronunciation threatening business also a corruption.

tunities states, this allows to them dictation your conditions.

corruption is impossible without it should also be taken into account. **existence of unregistered funds in the** country . In contrast, illegal **reduction in the number of** capital **issuances** and investments implemented **projects are indicators of instability and corruption in** banking . kov sector, irrational tax policy, deficiencies shield to indicate, to declare economic they come out.

The immorality of corruption also lies in the fact that corruption is enriching .ditch **carried out** immortality only back Control often irreplaceable resources however and, first of all, at the **expense of the** majority of **citizens** . Citizens and representatives who realize this witnesses business should in every possible way to support to fight with corruption.

4.8. Ways to combat administrative corruption Management corruption - most Widespread opinion

corruption _ small over dimensions degenerate offers, couple-

undercover over base and average levels authorities. Danger in it distribution awkwardness gradually discredits the system as a whole. sole cor- rupee (one from Species which? - Management corruption) a ba- animal formation more high school over level Species corruption.

Aim Management corruption - to create system personal enriched- trughthe use of their position in the system of state power . **strangeness phenomenon authorities is is in Sound, What he is contents- their life back Control monetary source of money citizens _ as taxpayers for**

which? and should hard.

roads decrease level Management corruption:

— Implementation of administrative reform to modernize conditions public service as well as the state structure The service, which is a complex institution, both according to the legal regulation. mental activity, Like this and system movements.

— Further differentiation and clarification of the functions of the policy sections chip to them basis instructions activities.

— optimization and modernization yield to indicate, to declare functions.

— Expanding the level of transparency of all government activities creation of the maximum possible transparency against the background of the servicevanilla completely civilian society.

— Expanding public control over state activities venous Services.

— creating systems "electronic state."

Public control will prevent, detect and eliminate. conditions, which? to contribute corruption and abuse over Go-to indicate, to declare service, increase quality and competence Work.

Overall, conversions should contribute to increasing efficiency. activities of state bodies. The main criterion for impact The efficiency of the public service should be welcomed. citizens (as consumers) finished Services.

COURSE 5. STRATEGY DEVELOPMENT PROVISIONS CORRUPTION HORSE REPUBLIC BELARUS

FEATURES APPROACH, EXPERIENCE And APPLICATIONS to fight

5.1. Level level corruption.

5.2. Vote tools for National fight corruption strategies.

5.3. Practical experience development and application fight corruption strategiesin Republic Belarus.

5.4. Place and role higher sizes executive and legislative authorities in about-social and political process application strategies opposition corruption.

5.5. Place and role source of money mass information in application fight corruptionnyh Events.

5.6. role business and public

organizations in formation and application national anti-corruption strategies.

5.7. Corruption in sphere Education.

5.1. Corruption in Sports.Level level corruption

corruption , above all, deep and inclusive analysis given phenomena. July immortality little, make all- third party evaluation level corruption sufficient complicated over reason Message- yanna dynamics. Quantity to fight and opposition corruption handle overhe is important coup in plan Changes units, level and forms.

Together with topics to be emphasize indirect marking manifestations post-natal stvia corruption as indicators, indicating over character availability, distribution peculiarities of corruption The presence of this indicator and the degree of its manifestation ditch in society maybe to indicate as over character corruption, Like this and over degreesuccess fight corruption quantity providing he is opposition.

Economic   Effects   manifestations

corruption:

— extension shady economy, decrease tax behave-lenia in to indicate, to declare budget;

— breach competitive mechanisms Market;

— insufficient use to indicate, to declare budget source of money;

— promotion final Price:%s Product:%s or Services;

— worsening investment climate.

Social Effects manifestations corruption :

— discrediting the law as the main regulatory instrument life states and society;

— abstraction to indicate, to declare source of money from targets public development, growing wealth inequality, substantial poverty Noah part of the population;

— strengthening organized crime, increase social Noah blood pressure.

political Effects manifestations corruption:

— shifting policy goals and objectives from national development thia with to ensure officials of corrupt groups;

— decrease trust with authorities, growth he is estrangement from society;

— drop prestige countries over International arena

— to reject political competition.

Like this path **Relatively to be to evaluate phenomenon over her after that-wiyam** and to determine degree expressionism her units, Species and forms.

It should be borne in mind that corruption in general is endangered. the scope of the rights and freedoms of all members of society, the protection of society education building, legitimacy and law and order in to indicate, to declare.

Corruption without goalkeeper opposition and amplification to fight with he isowner Real estate expand and develop Therefore fight corruption no function a one from basis functions none to indicate, to declare stva. Basis aim fight corruption politicians everybody states I'm in- ensure the protection of the rights and legitimate interests of citizens, society and empowering the state against threats from the effects and consequences of corruption, as well as lenia trust societies with to indicate, to declare and her institutions. This achievable only over basis in every way Research corruption and applications for stand- movements he is most effective and loyalty quantity coup.

5.2. Vote tools

for National fight corruption strategies

Anti-corruption measures can be divided into: groups. The first group **includes measures to combat** external manifestations .corruption (bribe special officers) already **existing blind-**

corruption, specific corruption officials, secondly - corporate nym prerequisites conditioning corruption **potential corruption**, if not that impersonal corrupt official under what conditions. It is also possible to go out alone pension quantity - **quantity over elimination results corruption _**

The first set of measures is punitive in nature, which means: zhaetsya in tightening state control. Some researchers Those who deal with the problem of corruption attribute such measures to one of the causes of corruption. corruption in developing countries Because of next Disadvantages:

— punitive measures widen the gap between profits nostalgic faces and level punishment potential corrupt official What and leads to with growth corruption;

— article lots quantity a myself corrupt officer, a immortality corruption;

— Finally, in frame data quantity with corruption between to indicate, to declare apparatus they are fighting exclusively representatives How are you today? device, What oftenthere you go in to fight against competitors over Market degenerate Services.

The second set of preventive measures is preventive, not punitive nature towards causes, not external expressions ny corruption, and therefore devoid of many deficiencies.

With quantity inhibitor character reference _ with example, security independence and competence judicial authorities; transparency in funded vanilla parties; transparency procedures voting for voters; absolute- the ability of officers to declare property; rules governing the subject conflict areas of interest; guarantee freedom information; to reject obstacle- ditch entrance over market, related with necessity taking various Once upon a time-decisions; venerable Payment labor to indicate, to declare employees; decentralization power concept; increase the transparency of the budget process to control cutting organs; increasing transparency in tax administration ,schenie tax employees opportunities arbitrarily to give tax-joyful privileges, simplification tax Administration.

should include improving legislation . **government and the legislative process** , for example, about instructions:

— withdraw money contradictions and explanation uncertainties in flow live state create possibility for bureaucratic arbitrariness and corruption;

— closing countless reference norms in existing laws;

— revision scales penalties back degenerate movements with taking into account To go, What often high priced punishment interfere evidence Crimes;differentiation degenerate movements;

— revision scales tasks, fines and etc.;

— squeezing control above department rule making;

— organisation fight corruption Expertise projects standard-nyh behaves.

one from important factors opposition

devastating affect over sustainable socio-economic development states, threatening Nationaladvance security Republic Belarus a one from **to indicate, to declare-Gmunte** effective implementation of state policy in the field of **anti-corruption programs** due to the need to fight with corruption. And Adoption lots kind fight corruption program will carried out and in Further forward.

programs in your name to make a decision the following mother **tasks** :

— to reject level degenerate crime;

— promotion competence activities law enforcementsizes in to fight with corruption;

— to win prosecution surveillance and to indicate, to declare control smooth fulfillment anti-corruption measures;

— creation productive mechanism prevention corruption.

Programs provide the solution of these

tasks measures to further improve legislation evidence over problems to fight with corruption with taking into account International experience as well as socio-economic and organizational practices practical Events anti-corruption character.

Programs **give an important place to the organization and target inspections in the most sensitive business areas corruption risks** . Among them, state-owned construction gift property at the expense of the budget appropriations provided leniye of residential buildings of the state housing stock, housing public services, provision of land by local authorities lands, supplies petroleum products and application Product:%s fuel-energy and petrochemistry complexes, credit and finance and banking, licensing of certain types of activities, fragmentation It was published material resources armed forces.Implementation of the activities of such state programs, prevent, detect and suppress corruption crimes demolition, strengthening fight against corruption systemic basis.

5.3. Practical experience in development and

implementation fight corruption strategies in Republic Belarus

ne of the components of an effective fight against corruption the existence of an appropriate legal framework (anti-corruption legislation), sufficient risk of corruption, andsystematically responding to all forms of corruption crimes no, a also reinforcement effective system precautionary and compensatory quantity directed over opposition corruption.

Currently, countermeasure issues in the Republic of Belarus action and anti-corruption within the national anti-corruption framework pearl legislation It is regulated by **laws** :"HE to fight in an organized way crime and corruption" (from 26 June 1997).

1. "HE to indicate, to declare service in Republic Belarus" (from fourteen June

2003 of the year).

2. "On measures to prevent the legalization of received income illegally" (July 19, 2000). new in 2005 oppression, which input in force in March 2006.

3. "HE declare physically persons Income, Real estate and resources Money" (from January 4 2003).

4. "On Anti-Corruption" (dated 20 July 2006). December 22, 2011 regular changes and additions were accepted and in April 2012 con entry in · force (application.).

Regulator legal actions Minister Republic Belarus:

— decree Minister Republic Belarus from 26 June 2001 g. Number. 20

"In the mandatory income and property declaration of the priority candidate Residents of the Republic of Belarus, their close relatives, spouses (additional friend) and his (his) parents and pro- conductive open, Free and fair elections.

— decree Minister Republic Belarus from nineteen April 2002 g. Number. eleven

"On the abolition of individual benefits for taxes, duties and customs duties on the improvement of the state support for the argument and the law persons and individual entrepreneurs."

– decree Minister Republic Belarus from thirty June 1995 g. Number. 244

"Problems of the Interdepartmental Commission on Combating Crime, rupee and drug addiction also Council Security Republic Belarus".

– decree Minister Republic Belarus from 2nd December 2000 g. Number. 577

"About some measures to improve working with personnel in the system to indicate, to declare organs."

– decree Minister Republic Belarus from 29 June 2001 g. Number. 358

"Organized Crime and Anti-Corruption Commission Issues time subordinate to the ministry interior."

– decree Minister Republic Belarus from 2nd October 2002 g. Number. 500

"HE to indicate, to declare program over

strengthening to fight with corruption over

2002 - 2006 years."

- decree Minister Republic Belarus from 23 September 2010 g. Number. 485

"On the State Program Against Crime and Corruption over 2010 – 2012".

— decree Minister Republic Belarus from 6 August 2003 g. Number. 347

"On certain matters concerning the statements of individuals tsami Income, Real estate and resources Money".

— decree Minister Republic from Belarus _ March 17 2004 no. _ 136 "HE former-trust management of shares owned by officers participation (shares, Rights) in legal source of money advertising organizations."

— decree Minister Republic Belarus from frontend September 2005 g. Number. 432

"HE a little quantity over Development organizations work with citizens-mi in to indicate, to declare bodies, other to indicate, to declare organizations about a little-ryh quantity over Development organizations work with citizens in to indicate, to declare donor bodies, other to indicate, to declare organizations."Other normative legal actions:

— Resolution of the Cabinet of Ministers of the Republic of Belarus of April 7 1994 No. For 217 "On organizational measures to strengthen the struggle against the former footsteps and corruption";

— Resolution of the Cabinet of Ministers of the Republic of Belarus of November 5 dream 2003 No. 1471 "On approval of the counter-action plan viyu corruption to indicate, to declare organs";

— decree plenum Sublime ships Republic Belarus from

26 June 2003 Number. 6 "HE judicial application over works about bribe";

Resolution of the Inter-Parliamentary Assembly of States Parties Commonwealth of Nations Independent states from fifteen November 2003 g. Number. 22-15 "HE moon logical live "Fundamentals legislation about fight corruption politics."

Anti-corruption legislation needs to be taken into account. her activities continually being improved.

The first action aimed directly at combating corruption time, it happened **Live Republic Belarus " oh to fight with crime in sphere again economy and corruption** » **1993 year** . Her arrangement diminished lots narrow definition phenomenon corruption and to create immortality- how much limitations and Requirements with public employees.

It was changed some time later and is now **in effect Republic of Belarus con "On combating organized crime and Corruption and Corruption,** which determines state policy in the fight against **corruption"** rupee, create organizational and legal basic knowledge lots combat.

The most advanced ideas **were embodied in the Law of the Republic of Belarus. russian "In the civil service in the Republic of Belarus" 2003** , established, affecting the causes of corruption most wide a circle limitations related with to indicate, to declare service.

Matter 22 live establishes ban for to indicate, to declare Employees:

1.1. Engaging in personal or business activities deductions from people trusted to help close relatives entrepreneurial activity using the picture Location, a also to be representative third persons over Questions, hardcover-

with the activities of the state body of which he is an employee. lyatsya or dependent and/or controlled he is.

1.2. Participate in management personally or through proxies nii business entity, unless otherwise stated- nyh legislation.

1.3. hold any other public office other than cases provided for by the Constitution of the Republic of Belarus, other legislators behaves.

1.4. To accept participation in strikes.

1.5. Engage in other paid work (activities) during office hours activity), except teaching, scientific, cultural, creative activities carried out in order and on the basis of medical practice love established by law.

1.6. fulfill work over conditions part time jobs, Moreover work in government institutions, in the determined manner and conditions legislation about labor.

1.7. Use official position for political interests parties, religious organizations, other legal entities and civil From, if This conflicting with areas of interest public service.

1.8. Do not accept any warnings from natural and legal persons legal rewards, including gifts in connection with with the performance of official duties, with the exception of souvenirs. By- radiant in Links with to apply formal responsibilities souvenir, cost exceeding the amount determined by the Government of the Republic which the Belarusian dimension is transferred to or used in state revenue in accordance with the procedure established by law (this amount has been determined for now) only in GK Republic Belarus in article 546 in format 5 basis quantities).

1.9. Use for personal purposes, free physical services and legal entities created by them in connection with the execution of the state nym employees their picture responsibilities.

1.10. Use of material tools for non-mission purposes technical, financial and information support, other creature government agency and official hidden.

1.11. Having an account in foreign banks, except for special cases performing government functions in other countries and in other countries viewed legislation cases.

1.12. to accept without the consent of the President of the Republic of Belarus, the statedonor foreign states.

Draft limitations a open. still WHO- the possibility of creating other restrictions at the legislative level nia, related with public service.

It also **provides for an officer's obligation. transfer to a trust in** accordance with a procedure established by law **management** under state guarantee for the duration of the state gift certificate Services **found in her Real estate shares participation** (shares, rights) in the authorized capital of commercial establishments niem cases envisaged legislation.

A lot **mechanism ingrained decree Minister Republic Belarus No. 136 of March 17, 2004** "On management of trust participation benefits (shares, rights-joyful) in legal funds of commercial organizations.

As a sanction for breach of these requirements, but the release of an officer from his post. violation wounds, related with to indicate, to declare service, a also one from ground termination public service (Art. 40 Live).

Article 23 of the Law provides for a citizen of the Republic of Belarus. when entering **public service** harvest - while occupying another public position as a resident legislative arrangement to be submitted to the **relevant state-** natural body **statement about Income and property** _

This procedure is established in the **Law of the Republic of Belarus "In December clarifying the property and income of individuals"** and in part otherwise - **by Decree of the President of the Republic of Belarus of June 26 2001 No. 20** "About mandatory income and property declaration The presidential candidate of the Republic of Belarus, his close relatives, spouse (wife) and her (his) parents and some other measures towards this committed to holding open, free and fair elections." Naru- schenie Requirements legislation also acceptance over to indicate, to declare service also speaking one from reason for this termination.

The next most important action in the fight against corruption Decree **500 of October 2, 2002,** ratifying **the state program for strengthening to fight with corruption** (Further forward - program).

By order administrations Minister Republic Belarus prepared and submitted to the House of Representatives of the National Assembly. **"Draft Law on Amendments and Additions"** of the Republic of Belarus **ny in Judicial and criminal procedure codes Republic**

Belarus over problems amplification responsibility back Crimes, associated with corruption. It aims to bring criminal law. Legislation of the Republic of Belarus in accordance with international norms foot Rights for questions prevention of corruption.

Judicial code Republic Belarus complete new article, to create responsibility back taking benefits non-proprietary character (acquisition formal face for myself or for third persons joyful-years non-proprietary character in format Services or promises advantage WA, provided exclusively in Links with busy to them formal location, back auspices or condone over service, convenientno decision Questions incoming in her sufficiency or back yield or default in areas of interest providing How are you today? use or representedto them that any action (inaction) that this person should haveor can handle with using they formal authority), frontlocation formal face bribe or benefits non-proprietary character- ra, providing benefits non-proprietary character.

According to paragraph 11 of the program, a (by Decree cited above) procedure for transition to trust management contributions (shares, rights) owned by civil servants legal advertising organizations.

Criminal liability according to the legislation of the Republic of Belarus Russia is **provided for** such acts of **corruption** . international law understanding and loyalty from selfish or different personal attention, as:

— abuse strength or formal forces (Art. 424 h. 2nd);

— inactivity formal faces (Art. 425 h. 2nd);

— EXTREME authorities or formal forces (Art. 426 h. 2nd);

— formal forgery (Art. 427);

— illegal participation in entrepreneur activities (Art. 429);

— taking bribe, in Sound including back commission illegal movements

(inaction) (Art. 430);

— cottage bribe, in including back commission illegal movements (without-

movements) (Art. 431);

— mediation in bribe (Art. 432);

— illegal remuneration by government employees pearl body or different to indicate, to declare organizations (Art. 433);

— legalization ("laundering") material values, Purchased-nyh judicial by (Art. 235).

5.4. Place and role higher sizes executive

and legislative power in the socio-political process application strategies opposition corruption

fight corruption politics centre and regions republics finalize- etya in developing and application multidirectional and consecutive quantity over elimination (minimization) reasons and conditions, productive corruption in different areas of life. Development and implementation of anti-corruption tasks politicians caps all levels legislative and executive authorities.

corruption without constant opposition feature to expand, it is necessary to highlight the anti-corruption function tion states as somebody her basis tasks.

Speech to go as about creation mechanisms, to let decrease the scale of corruption and development and developing a strategic anti-corruption policy on a permanent basis The growing organic function of the state. At the same time, the efficiency the function will largely depend on how active it is. legislative, executive strength and civil society structures.

Corruption of the executive branch **etya Sound** Done **unnecessary** to indicate, to declare **functions** , **do a suboptimal incentive structure for** government employees **reap** _ Thus, the improvement of the authorization system presses important reserve for level reduction corruption.

For increase competence to indicate, to declare to manage

should Draw Attention over owner Location:

— short level performance disciplines;

— prevalence of undesirable 'gouging' situations Instructions and arbitrary establishment order to them yield;

— orientation over department interest;

— poor motivation for the activities of civil servants (op-Salaries of civil servants are not directly related to the results of their work. activities);

— blurring of decision-making criteria in the absence of open obligations former society and leadership;

— extreme centralization forces over acceptance Answers.

Therefore, **a package of anti-corruption measures in the public sphere public administration** may include work related to: shchim instructions:

1. elimination situations conflict they come out.

2. Increase abilities sizes authorities put and To succeed what-one of both, in Sound including back Control project management.

3. Arrangement activities sizes authorities and standardization to them interactions with citizens.

4. Formalization representative office areas of interest in sizes authorities.

5. formation electronic forms appeal and return documents.

6. creating "electronic state."

7. Security conditions transparency activities political steam- ty and election campaigns for society.

Necessary immortality to be angry application principle separation keep state-level powers and executive within authorities. Strict classification of authorities, division of powers to them should to base over medicine function is performed.

It should be noted that the division of functions in itself does not imply an automatic answer to the question of interests. transfer of functions to the non-state sector. solution in this direction should be considered on a case-by-case basis. Same timeorganizational separation of functions allows you to start the optimization process the provision of public services by identifying the potential no situations and potential objects.

Separation functions will provide:

1) to be saved from Corporate conflict areas of interest;

2) to identify fields transfer functions and Get out yield themor other operations back limits states;

3) increase competence to manage back Control cuts Shack-definite control.

A mechanism needs to be introduced .nisms Payment labor, over Results substantially growing variable Section wage fees officers and connecting he is taking with truth achievements what-left values over topics or otherwise delivered former body authorities targets. It is the overall effective strategic management process that minimizes conditions for corruption, includes in myself definition next parameters:

— mission (explanation need existence body authorities);

— purpose (future state of social relations, which? Section guides your efforts)

— performance indicator (not in terms of sectors, No parameters target groups);

— targeted values indicators (For example, increase satisfactorily resolution body services authorities 20 %).

In the system of state branches of power and international public structures had feedback mechanisms zi (use of information from grading achievement of the determined targets, effectiveness of the developed programs,evaluation of the results by the public, evaluation of its feasibility legislative Answers level arrangement them or other tasks).

Thus , **the level of participation of the legislative and executive Authorities in the fight against corruption and the fight against corruption, strategic planning** and includes in myself identification targeted groups citizens, assessment of the external environment of the activities of the authorities. The case of strategic mangment allows us to consider the functions of organs . authorities in context owner mine mission instructions to them activities, ori- focused, everybody over her level, over satisfaction areas of interest citizens.

5.5. The place and role of mass media in application fight corruption Events

The fight against corruption is a hot topic, not just in bodies. not only in the media, which is explained by the use of the media as an element. providing systemic countermeasure and the fight against corruption. By media information about fight corruption activities executiveand the legislatures of the government reach out to the society and disseminate the media. acknowledging the results and reflecting society's view of its effectiveness. possible measures to combat it. It's just that society and the state to interact effectively about it, but also to fix it VAT system Measures taken.

should be noted that **no matter how important solutions to specific problems, improved measures** or ideas, calculated without the consequences **being disseminated and discussed in society. they will remain outside the scope of implementation, they will remain** just ideas individual To let highly competent peoples.

At the same time, the **media** is not just an **information channel.** scrap with reverse Contact **between to indicate, to declare and society** . These hard and **conductors formation in society** strategic **ideologies**

fight corruption, create a climate not his As Yatiya phenomena and forms of relationship. Under what conditions does the media conservative fight corruption societies acquires real features over- a rational system of its own that gains stability he is foundations of inner beliefs citizens.

Thus, the role of the media in enforcing anti-opposition corrupt apps cannot be overestimated. On the one hand, without Prevention and fight against corruption by mass media is impossible. Along with the other - **media representatives should highly value their status** and to carry out their duties, as their job is to **provide**

information material and information security in the countermeasures system acts of corruption and the fight against it . It is unacceptable when they are media workers are involved in high-profile corruption scandals, What discredit principle public control.

Own role in implementing anti-corruption measures can play not only individual representatives of media genres, but also their creators ski collectives, as well as their public associations. creative unions representatives of press, television and radio companies, Journalists' Union etc. moon bowel develop ethic codes of types activities.

fixation and Spread truths corruption and bribe between rowing buildings, I'm talking in quality inhibitor quantity over relationship with moon peersthe mentally unstable from committing corruption Actions that contribute to the participation of non-governmental organizations in the fight against corruption society, together with topics immortality should get dressed character ill-conceived systems.

HORSE system quantity undertaken **in opposition and to fight corruption,** established by the state and must be observed **moral, ethical and legal principles adopted in society,** only **predetermining their civilized forms opposition corruption,** however **and public support** in Generally.

A lot principles are:

— Legality.

— Justice.

— equality all former by law.

— Promotion.

— inevitability responsibility.

— Personal guilty responsibility.

— humanism.

The media, on the one hand, under the auspices of the executive branch, effective financial groups, on the other hand, are trying to increase the volume of freedom of expression and "advertisement variation. It is unacceptable to intensify the mass media mating in the hands of oligarchs when minorities Even exposure corruption used quality to fight for strength.

hour all multidimensionality preferences and balance areas of interest mother The task of the media is the creation of rational consciousness: consumer Trustworthy information. HORSE otherwise situation inevitably WHO- nickle do not misunderstand between strength and society. What maybe to be and conclusion-tattoo Changes Because of development society, stabilization which? tre bouquet immortality only efforts however and moral solvency, enlightenment and shelf conscience [HE. Spengler; L. n. Gumilev].

5.6. role business and public organizations

in formation and application fight corruption strategies

The complexity of the fight against corruption in different countries, from the point of view of citizens, lies in the fact that the **fight against corruption is carried out by them. incoming in category representatives power** _ July most subconsciouslypeople immortality quite a few trust process How are you today? to fight. problem a and he istruth, What face, in your name to ensure fit legality, often themselves need in supervision What is is yourself "closed a circle".

An important factor for an effective fight against corruption is high moral authority is needed, such as that of a top manager Leading leaders of all branches of leadership and government. What- One of the most important elements in the fight against corruption really large scales usually exactly higher eshe- power wombs. Fighting corruption at this morale level action is not enough. Legal Sanctions and Required Sanctions compliance with corruption laws. If such sanctions against rupee immortality available, them should be introduced.

But the problem is that in some states corrupt leaders who are also legislators,to adopt appropriate laws to combat corruption, so that we M former Total, protect yourself.

Therefore, **one of the main problems hindering its impact is the** effective **fight against** corruption, who comes first, Total, **should lead** How are you today? **fight**.

Corruption, as it is closely related to the activities of representativesto indicate, to declare authorities, endowed with definite forces, back thenIf there is corruption in this environment, it is difficult to expect it. to indicate, to declare strength will be decided given problem.

Creation of multiple state structures (control control) engaged in the fight against corruption, does not just solve trouble, but exacerbate it. **The increase in the number of** controllers, censor, control, and authorize **state structures** it simultaneously **increases the number of officials** and **creates conditions. not to exclude personal interests from their** officers provisions. hour How are you today? themselves representatives "check" sectors In fact, it has been taken out of the control of society, which is full of dangers in itself. back then more big extension corruption.

Analytical material of sociological research

on the problem corruption indicates a violation of anti-corruption requirements. legislation and ethic principles activities partner side employeesto create in society psychological Income ingenious to create system from more complex problems. Thus **the idea of conceptual struggle tackling corruption as** a complex issue **with he is should** inclusive means and, former Total, **forces citizens-sky society,** using also How are you today? lots mechanisms, as creation independent these non-governmental organizations, independent funds media , strengthening the independence of the judiciary, to who dissemination local self management.

To eradicate corruption, only a single legal effort. It should not be forgotten that success in the fight against corruption depends, first of all, on the active participation of the population in this process. **Number of people whose rights were violated due to corruption employees lots more these persons** .

To change the situation, people need to realize their legal rights. control activity formal persons, receive possibility Access to reports on the expenditure of public funds, check them professionalism and moral qualities, taking part in salvation research institutes from negligent and dishonest employees.

The provision that the civil servant is the servant of the people ,Wage worker, it is not enough to write laws, it is important **to implement into people's minds to** feel empowered . responsible lords of the country.

Countries that have had the best success in fighting corruption special next properties:

— small dimension states;

— open separation legislative, managerial and con- trawl duties of officials;

— creation in country conditions for activities completely independentwe are X and free funds mass information;

— creation conditions for Free economic activities.

One of the important issues

determining success in the field of wrestling with corruption a to create priority instructions combat.

the simplest Suggestions in combat with corruption has in the hardening of criminal liability for its manifestations. Meanwhile, the extreme **severity of** punishment is not an effective solution. **casing** How are you today? kind **crimes** .

States with stable democratic traditions highly effective and time-tested **political ways** to limit the negative manifestations of corruption among those who are not which? from occupation formal shipments persons.

With most effective from to them valid **to indicate, to declare device, established over wide dissemination self management citizens and What-rhyodic selectivity persons,** endowed with authoritarian forces.

The principle of separation of powers with its mechanism checks and counterweights also obstacles concentration authorities in a little RU-kah. It is also very important that this system has an independent structure.and unbiased court, enjoy respect and trust population.

Practice has shown that it is unfavorable for the abuse of moisture. atmosphere **of openness** and freedom of expression, independent free media, transparency for society systems of social payments and guarantees for vulnerable groups of the population nia in conditions socially oriented economy.

economic field, then to win corruption, it is necessary to transfer the economy to the "market tracks", promotion of free enterprise, competition, multi-layered economy, limitation intervene strong buildings in economic

relationships. It is necessary to create favorable conditions for development. Ensuring private initiative, transparency and accountability society public use Real estate.

In general, **the solution to the corruption problem can only be the basis of an integrated approach, taking into account the** results of integrated scientific research nyh **Research and to work positive experience** many countries.

Anti-corruption activities cannot be effective in the following situations: isolated from society and run only by civil servants. mi. And in this fight for a better future, responsibility comes first. first of all, to the citizens of each country and above all to initiatives nyh and responsible representatives civilian society.

As initiative links in society, businessmen be outside the fight against corruption. anti-corruption activities, protect their interests and affect their economic efficiency. mimics the activity. Income also depends on the amount of tax deductions. states. July most suitable active participation business message society as an initiative element of an organized civil society in all measures of consolidated anti-corruption measures, qualified formation they positions over problem corruption.

5.7. Corruption in sphere Education

HORSE various countries systems Education being built over various principlecipach, in to them structure in toy or different measurement to present managers caused- necessary structures, has its own characteristics and systems. relationships in to them. School in process Education gets important meaning. School- Tïsyte is less prone to corruption than other areas . But often corrupttime starts with reception kids in first classes big cities, there, where there possibility vote schools. Often problem climbing topics factor WhatMany children have reached different levels of preschool education. Many ro-parents understand What quality teaching and pedagogical talent con-special teachers maybe substantially affect over destiny to them children. strugglesign up in the best schools and classes, created competitive conditions, What th-Vato tries to corruptly impress them. Eliminate such situationsperhaps by improving the quality of education in general, but is is yourself sufficient complicated and long process.

HORSE universities most process owner they features, where all rowing actualditch effects over possibility formation degenerate relationships. Head-nym factor to them eliminate in many countries serves system action over corruption prevention. For example, the Ministry of Education Republic Belarus in frame systems quantity over warning corruption sent to heads of higher educational educan organizations letter " On the implementation of **anti-corruption legislationand** ". HORSE given document outside Instructions a also reminders articleAccording to teachers and students of the Criminal Code of the Republic of Belarus meek May to be included with judicial responsibility, in application had given titles universities and lists names teachers and students, hardcover-nyh with degenerate relationships.

factors ingenious make sure effective oppositioncorruption in universities must be taken into account: an increase in ideological level bots, high quality staff selection and training, ad hoc creative creation ski collectives with the participation of students; create conditions for application of scientific ideas; interaction with the practical field; created- new specialties and fields of study; level detection salaries from quality and units Work, collection teaching increase the prestige of teams, teaching and research activities, responsibility for tasks performed, assigned government grants for the development and participation of creative youth he is in creative labor and scientific activity.

5.8. Corruptio in sports

The danger of the manifestation of corruption in the field of sports lies in the fact that: that corrupt relationships do not only manifest on a professional level. sional sports, but affects children's and youth sports. h- not only do we undermine creative interest in the beginning potential athletes' self-actualization, which is also unacceptable my atmosphere development these species Sports.

In some countries, children's sports schools instead of separate make sure physically and spiritual development they students, asand attracting young people to socially beneficial activities, the goal is not to create conditions for sports achievements, creation over How are you today? basis business relationship systems. relationships in sports sphere and sports organizations return in institutions

commercial type whose interests are not compatible with its actual development sport, as a result, the foundations of organization and form- english sustainable development for all Species Sports.

An example How are you today? May hard cases, when? has treaties over free education of children in a sports school. However, sports inventory, sports format and travel over sports Events and fees parents give account immortality only pay back mine Control, however and to notice In addition additional fees over Requirements coaching persons.

System originally created for commercialization of education directly affect the formation of the personality of athletes, character and content sports results in Generally.

no doubt What Even first preparation athlete owner mine price.However speech to go, former Total, immortality only about formation sports elite, however and about mass Sports, supportive in active physically ingenious bigzhdan countries. Should think,

What hanging interest with sports providing no health nation and he is the future generations without important costs.

Establishment unnecessarily high school Price:%s (under encase care about read-Share) over participation in mass child and youth Sports, Even also to know-rigorous Caution partner side states with sports and availability sufficient number of sports facilities, often outside the sports ground important quantity potential athletes immortality to let over first-name scene make sure systemic identification most talented from to them.

HORSE mine order unfilled sports spheres renews judicialnou. This shows the degree of danger of corruption in sport, systematically weakening basic knowledge well-being societies and states.

The danger of corrupt relationships in the professional field sports is is in Sound, What in How are you today? sphere meet people immortality interested bathrooms in sports Results and prestige countries. These immortality too much to stay behind bye areas of interest commands, clubs, respectfully be interested with athletes and Bo-dear, however to actualize personal enrichment back to them Control.

hour How are you today? lots kind interest immortality annoyed one or many- mi coaches, players and a little number other persons. How rule coverage- promise yourself all system (rice. 5.1)). July most Sport It is possible, over rowing her industries, sphere degenerate activities, owner politicized OS- new, in Sound including - over level International political corruption.Rice. 5.1. system corruption sphere sports

Supposedly used today. "sports pharmacology" too much areas of interest development Sports, how much her demolition. systems service to want anti-doping tracing immortality in ingenious in complete measurement embrace allsports spheres and topics most make sure expired control.

Appearance only in end past sports Rights to let Chef frames for take ownership National areas of interest athletes and over-rational sports over International level also shows over importantno limitations in given sphere, Used corrupt officials for applied-tion they selfish tasks.

Materials appear very often in the media they express. doubts about the "objectivity" of the outcome of sporting events (matches, fights, races, etc.) People who stand out rarely do not fall under suspicion. sports stars and clubs, coaches. The reason is true This world sport has not only become more popular in recent years, but also and advertising, inevitably being article degenerate activities.

The growth of professionalism, both in the playgrounds and beyond - coverage of ongoing competitions in the media, sponsorship and a large ny Market sports odds in America, Asia and Europe returned The evolution of sports into a multi-billion-dollar industry is often precisely what equestrian received reached.

Corruption in sports in Generally - phenomenon International and think-VAT her in scale one countries not practical. Big Market conflict- active odds actively develops, and often makes participants gamblinggames, which? role play, in Sound number, and effective judicial structure-ry, handle coup over Results sports Events.

Availability of a contract activity

primarily associated with sports With the growth of the betting industry. Bookmakers are growing faster than others Markets in Asia, Eastern Europe and Scandinavia. In Russia, as in Russia others countries Peace, high school to step develops Like this in your name

"Sports Market".

Both are provided by the legislation of the Russian Federation (Article 184 of the Criminal Code of the Russian Federation) and the Republic of Belarus (Article 253 of the Criminal Code of the Republic of Belarus) criminal liability for bribing exhibitors and professional organizers logical Sports competitions.

However, the vast majority and not just sports shifts, coaches, sports referees etc., but also law enforcement organizations are often unaware that these articles may be relevant. nims to participants and organizers of professional sporting events acceptance. And the composition of this crime is highly la- tents. Back Crimes this kind prisoner only units.

Cause bribe sports referees serves also insufficient professionalism employees specialized in fields to fight with frontfaulty qualification in the field of economic activity title deed, existing legal, organizational and operational search means To upload and find out guilty face.

Identification economic Crimes is is insignificanta fraction of the total number of crimes committed, but in sports In other areas, as a rule, it is even lower. What fact does it point to At the moment, the seriousness of the current situation is not fully understood. situations and topics most immortality given expired Caution How are you today? problem.

In addition, existing methods of combating economic crimes films in the field of sports should borrow from foreign experiences countries wrestle with corruption in this area.

In particular, the creation of investigation departments will be of great importance. relationships in sports federations that can significantly reduce Number of match-fixing and other crimes in the professional field advance Sports.

Effective measures to combat current crime are their special services in sports festivals operating around the world. regions where former law enforcement officers worked organs. However, pre-crime in the field of sports would be the establishment of a sports police and its active cooperation with Interpol and Europol.

It is clear that interest in this field is growing from the side. states and societies, national law enforcement agencies It can reduce the crime rate in the field of sports. But for the radical Any solution to corruption problems in this area is a broad International and professional cooperation relating to sections and Services, ingenious make sure Effect over basis Contact plexo and coordinated measures.

DICTIONARY

Agency relationship - relationship between employees kami and Administration. Agency behaviour a central to connect-agent theories on which theoretical explanations are based rupee. Management taken into account in quality owner, a workers - as agents. However, this standard approach is a simplification. nym. If the establishment is financed from the state budget, at the expense of it taxpayer funds, then the relationship between the state and the organization It is also an agency relationship. Individual employees and managers Many organizations are also intermediaries, especially tasked with assessing their qualifications and professional qualifications. howling faces. In this case, they can betray the interests of their owners. case - society, if they provide low quality service and are rewarded to unfairly impart professional qualifications without the appropriate professional mental skills. This approach broadens the scope of the concept.agency interactions in the various areas where corruption occursrelationships.

Academic corruption includes nonsense

major and illegal acts and operations, including illegal ones means attitude towards the educational process: biased assessment girl information, undeserved taking diplomas, allowance qualifications plagiarism, failure to provide scientific guidance, violation of research ethic, data tampering.

Also, the use of "dead souls" found in organizations formally, in the form of workbooks; biased evaluation of individuals when recruiting work or advancement on the academic and career ladder. this type corruption, unintended construction, profit- irrational or inappropriate public use of sports venous financing etc.

Academic neglect is a form of criticism. small or illegal behaviour artists and Administration. This form of neglect, especially in education, responsible behaviour, ignore they responsibilities reflecting low quality teaching (unreadiness for classes, old materials, refusal from participation in educational and methodical studies).

Anonymous telephone lines - telephone lines arranged by the administration to collect information about illegal measured and corrupt actions of employees. The information received is advertisement- Administration also Help anonymous phone lines, Used for concessions objectionable employees found in conflict with executive-Radio. Usually anonymous phone lines are not set up to fight but to apply administrative pressure and get rid of corruption objectionable.

Asymmetric information - characterizes a situation that signals about illegal and corrupt offer services and bribes available in corrupt market not reaching potential social customers and buyers not enough Clear or immortality mating. Asymmetric information is one of the key features of coordination. rupee market. The reason for the asymmetry of information flows, lies in the illegal nature of corruption. Fear of risk and punishment together with cultural properties to contribute hiding information about corruption or misrepresentation. As a result, the transaction Corruption costs in the corruption services market may exceed average Action costs in a particular industry. Also, some corruption rational Services May has been offered over high priced Price:% p.

obstacles for events over Market (Entrance obstacles) - set Charter including regulations and restrictions set by government and organizations to regulate access to certain industries to represent the professions and markets. obstacles for events has one from key character-the bat of the corrupt industry. a particular part of the national economy maybe organized to indicate, to declare and to ensure need licensedvaniya and accreditation. Barriers to market entry encourage development corruption between formal persons, responsible back licensing and accredited tation More To go, themselves organizations providing Services often to useServices to indicate, to declare officers for achievements and to continue half monopoly positions in local service markets to gain additional snow. Certification documents retrieval system, testing no, delivery exams and etc. - classical example facilities obstacles and annoyed ny in Entrance, create basis for corruption.

Baksheesh is an oriental term meaning reward. gift, offer or bribe. paid to various evaluation members good grades in exchange for commissions, referrals, teachers, or offers from grateful customers.

Favoritism is the practice of giving undeserved favors. shortcomings and priorities to individual customers by violating established rules pitchfork and professional and ethical standards. Kindness or favoritism is characteristic establishes a special positive relationship based on kinship, friendship, personal relationships. sympathy and others distinguishing features.

Tip - bribe paid after a fix tearing action. Gratitude is actually a form of pushback, but persecuted over live.

break out (chronism) - special, positive behaviour, carried outAdministration with definite persons and colleagues over basis related, friendly or other relations and violation of established rules. Recognition-that and manifestations blade to be to explore practically in all spheres.

Bureaucracy (Bureaucracy) - almost all employment, including administrative Radio organizations, face, responsible back development, control and audit special

Noah's field of activity. Since these employees are people who accept decision makers are therefore susceptible to the lure of corruption and opportunities implementation of corruption schemes.

Mutual benefit (Reciprocity) is the main principle of corrupt swap. Mutual benefit is based on a proportional exchange; parties extracts additional benefit.

A bribe is any value used in an exchange between two people. parties to an illegal transaction. Bribes are not necessarily paid in cash. and can be in the form of any tangible and intangible value, including assets and services. Intended to act as an incentive to bribe responsible desired Answers homeowner bribe in use to give bribe.

Briber - the person or organization giving the bribe, i.e. both- protector, offers.

Bribery (Bribe) - an official who takes a bribe, i.e. most- accepts the promise of a bribe, the offer of a bribe, or the bribe itself. Management, as well as authorized and decision-making persons. same employees control and governing organizations taken into account in quality bribe takers.

Corrupt practices (Bribe) - term, Used for assignmentsphenomenon huts and taking bribe. Corrupt practices often perceived in kahonour synonym corruption, however term corruption lots more wide Receive-precision also accepted think most influential naked for-mine corruption. On the contrary over judicial and Management responsibility,envisaged in legislation many countries, corrupt apps a everyday reality and is perceived as something ordinary, normal. HORSE addictions from countries, a little forms bribe May to be delivered outside live, in back then time as other forms bribe quite a few le-gallon and Even immortality taken into account in quality bribe or Something illegal. complexity National industry, including level price- trawl, Coordination, control, monetary Live Broadcasts, legislation, business structures and labor relationships to create difficulties in Diagnostics

and discovery corruption.

Cost is one of the determining factors. shchih drive forces corruption. If one attributed costs workers low back then organizations accept low wages but complement it. collect bribes and others illegal purchases

externalities are inevitable. People It works kinds activities has public good. The way services are created and distributed predetermines the existence of external services. third party related Effects.

Hostile takeover - a situation an organization is in nization to expand opportunities for corruption hostile to it, for example direct competitors or other alternate owners to carry out a hostile takeover, and clutch.

Medical fraud - takes place in medical centers, outpatient clinics and hospitals. Medical forgery includes in myself necessity Payment back Services, immortality privileged patient extract patients which? need in further forward treatment, falsification medical records, extract recipes over medicines, instructions and References in swap over bribe, embezzlement source of money from money source, government medical programs, etc. is financed by Weak control by the state, corruption of officials, to shout supervision back activities medical institutions, protection organizations they degenerate doctors lead with further forward growth corruption.

Second chance (the benefit of doubt) is wrong and confusing. The concept of behavior of the controlling body, the manager, consists of tags to lure a potential customer. First, it is possible the ability to break certain rules without warning of the consequences, and submission of a report to the body dealing with the assessment of such a situation; demolition.

profit is the practice of making a profit. legally or in violation of the organization's core purposes. Especially Universities sometimes forget their functions of producing and transferring knowledge. do research and teaching, focus on profitability benefit activity boards. As a rule, compressing profitshigh school, does not manage without violations laws and corruption.

extinguisher source of money (siphoning closed) - one) application "soft" embezzlement background- beat. Government funds initially listed for direct funding english and conductive Research, result in Used immortality over ration-nyu or stolen. Often vote and translation source of money carried out Officials already promised commissions and aware of the possibility hidden reproductive and withdraw money source of money by wrong applications about Sound budback then to want Completed Works.

2) Creation by authorities of regional or national systems topics Requirements from workers taking to them immortality caused necessity and

content of secondary or additional higher education activities with a formal administrative and legal basis for this process. In contrast, this type of paid additional higher education, a source of income shared among those participating in a corruption scheme We (university ⁇ Administration).

Extortion (extortion) - necessity bribe with application threats.

Horizontal corruption - a form of organization corruption where bribery and other illegal purchases are collected In contrast to the hierarchical order, individuals are individually and independently of each other. corruption.

graft (graft) - total collected bribe.

To make pressure partner side colleagues (Peer To make pressure) - or partner side set - characterizes the negative impact that corrupt officials have on their collaborators.lie down in highly corrupt organizations, many people, become involved in corruption otherwise their business or other purchases and privileges.

Double monopoly - characterizes the situation, When both sides of the negotiation have a monopoly position. Typical A double monopoly occurs when a citizen can: you read permission or service only also definite faces.

Discrimination - gender, nationality, race, nationality, social status, political opinion are corruption he is. Price discrimination immortality a format corruption in society.

theses - writing practice and Preparation for the defense of theses carried out by a non-scientific degree applicant, a professionals over order, or Like this in your name "niggers". HORSE a little country theses for sale or theses to order up to a third account from number of all protected.

donor (donor) - face, to give bribe.

Reaching entry age common practice when individuals periodically bring their children to work children, nieces and grandchildren to show them to their colleagues and who path guarantee to them acceptance over Work.

Friendly thesis boards - dissertation councils ready to accept a low quality thesis for defense or "close your eyes" to the fact that the thesis submitted for defense has been written dignity not by the applicant himself, but by order. perform such protections in return. in exchange for patronage, as well as bribes and other illegal offers local administrations and others sizes to indicate, to declare to manage.

Annual market volume – calculated corruption vaetsya as all Sound bribe, data in swap over unsuitable preferences and beneficiaries for a given year.

Documented evidence is facts that form the evidence base for corruption in government institutions management and other organizations. Evidence basis for corruption costs from matchless employee hidden operational video shooting, protocols and court decisions, news from official sources of information. documents Evidence of corruption should not be confused with perceptions of corruption. population. Perception of corruption by population and individual groups is revealed in interviews and opinion polls. Inter- opinion and opinion polls, both anonymous and public, has documented evidence corruption.

salaries - taken into account It is considered as the most important factor affecting the level of corruption. tion between them.

record in universities over basis testing (Scale based acceptances) - them. overbasis Results independent testing, or Unified to indicate, to declare e.gswap, a competitive format revenues in universities. HORSE a little countries back- numbering in universities over basis testing summoned to obstruct development degenerate-tion also acceptance over budget Location.

Non-competitive bidding is a form of corruption owner Location also breach hold giving an offer back contracts and contracts. As a result of violations, competition rules are not followed and contract prices chiki is not the most acceptable. Guidance on the road corruption limits the number of bidders and gives preference. to their wards. Bidding problem is often identified to beat the competition leaves conflict they come out.

Hierarchical corruption - a form of organization bribes and other illegal gifts collected partially or wholly directed from subordinates to superiors Wu passed several levels. Hierarchical corruption provides: difference vertical degenerate authorities.

Selective (selective) **justice** (Selective justice) - representing This is the practice of selective punishment of corrupt officials. degenerate Organizations, layoffs threaten non-corrupts most inconvenient for employees and management. Loyalty is considered as the main criterion for the selection of reliable employees. To beat-effective justice is also individual or organizations, immortality supportive sovereign political elite.

costs - losses for society, total the harm caused to society by corruption. Besides being economical losses due to knowingly wrong decisions, low professionalism and loss human capital, losses from corruption include moral destruction. values, pessimism, cynicism, insecurity and social There is no connection. Losses due to corruption should be calculated taking into account the long-term risks. As the negative consequences of corruption manifest itself, ten years later, having a cumulative negative impact on future generations, society and the state in Generally.

intensity corruption (Corruption intensity) - calculated as The average number of numbers issued or accepted in a given period of time, per year, for example, per one corruption officer who gives or receives bribe. The intensity of corruption in some organizations, to others, despite the fact that there may be an average size of bribery in them below. As a result, it is possible for organizations to be at a higher level. ness corruption May in After all save less quantity bribe.

Use of the state (takeover of the State) - literally, "takeover of the state stva" is the degree of influence of institutions on the state and de facto privatization. in relation to particular organizations within the functions of the state itself use. State use includes lobbying organization- state bodies. Lobbying is a legalized form corruption. Organizations compete with each other for access to the public. allocation of funding through funds, preferences, and government bribery gift officials and politicians. Use of government agency- We serve in response to attempts to increase government influence and control. above to them.

Cartel (Cartel) - a group of several organizations involved secret drinker to gain control over a particular segment services market. They can be promoted through the organization of cartels. their income through unreasonable price increases the law does not which? countries cartels forbidden a to them

Education maybe acceptable in quality forms of manifestation corruption.

Product quality (Product quality) - usually clarified. The corrupt scheme for obtaining a product is distinguished by its ambiguity. laziness.

Kleptocracy is a system run by criminals. employees who collect bribes and are involved in embezzlement of funds; and Real estate organizations. kleptocracy - system unofficially approved and approved corruption.

customer service (customer) - characterizes format social organizations, also which? definite faces have definite privilege and endowed with kiss-

certain advantages over others. Privileges Data received in exchange for bribes or the right of family or friendship. shiny customer service available and between central and local, arrangement ruminant and control to indicate, to declare bodies.

Customer risk (Fiduciary risk) - degree possibilities violations Officers know their powers and responsibilities. On workers and hell The administration is held responsible for the transactions it carries out and the transactions it performs. quality. Employees involved in corruption violate their obligations fulfill its obligations and mislead the society, the state and others. owl side.

codes - a set of rules that govern Professional behavior in organizations. The Code of Ethical Conduct reflects: professional values, the rules set by the state and consumer responses. Defines the scope of what is allowed in professional organizations. organizations.

Ethics committee - a committee of individuals and advertising - The ministry claims it is investigating corrupt activities. To go- government agencies also appoint similar commissions for investigation purposes. vanilla corruption in to indicate, to declare buildings.

Competitive bribery - a form of organization bribery in which employees partially copy each other's functions. Competition between workers leads to with decrease middle size bribe, a trace- more importantly, with cheaper degenerate Services, rising to them availability, and grown-he is users degenerate Services.

rivalry formal faces (Competition officers) - employees and other formal face, who's? forces in a little degree matchor is duplicated.

Controlled corruption - corruption, regulation hum to indicate, to declare authorities or leadership organizations. Arrangement includes control level corruption, mother and minority forms corruption. controlled corruption immortality means corruption over low level.

Hidden phone lines - these are phone liner, organized Administration with aim To collect information about the corrupt practices of employees. information obtained through anonymous phone lines sometimes used to compromise conflicts with management. Hidden phone lines it can often be organized not to fight corruption but to enforce it. stvlenie get rid of administrative pressure and objectionable. This form taking information often creates visibility absence need in circulation with law enforcement authorities. **Conflict of interest** - characterizes the following situations: an employee is solving a self-interested problem interest. In such cases, self-interest may intervene. allowing a person or manager to carry out their duties with an open mind and properly touchingly. Influential government officials be in a conflict of interest. A conflict of interest pre- suspicion and violation professional ethics.

Corporate takeover characterizes hostility debt absorption. A corporate takeover may include:goals: elimination of competitors, expansion, use of organizationstrademark, good reputation as "umbrella" or "umbrella" roofs to obtain accreditation.

Corrupt - recipient of bribes or other benefits, semi- chennyh illegal. A corrupt official is an official with an authority. limited authority and authority stnym location in use bribe giver and gets back This bribe. Corruption is not limited to bribery and therefore not only bribe recipients lyayutsya corrupt officials.

Degenerate covering (Corruption coverage) - Share producers and consumers of the field of activity, i.e. managers, doctors, assistant staff, patients involved in corruption, whatever form, form We, and the result degenerate situation.

Corruption in college athletics The place of the athletes in the systems that they have to pass through the sports system, to be considered as applicants for professional positions national sports clubs. Federations are profiting sports competitions and, accordingly, registration of athletes back Control abilities, a with taking into account sports potential.

Corruption in higher education - the system matter of informal relations for the purpose of unauthorized regulation access to material and moral benefits through abuse forces, authorized society, to indicate, to declare, or company.

Corruption in higher education manifests itself in the following ways: corruption in access to higher education, including violations at the national level testing and unified state exams, during violations entrance exams and bribery; corruption in research, including Violation of tea research rules, deliberate misrepresentation results, data tampering, forgery, plagiarism and corruption. when receiving and using research grants; corruption in education vocative process, including low quality teaching, return diplomas

professional suitability, fraud, plagiarism, collusion, forgery seals, manufacture, distribution, sale and counterfeit use diplomas, organization of diploma factory, sale and use of academic documents custom-made works; corruption in higher education administration vane, including imaginary teachers and pay them wage fees, waste and misuse of budget funds, buildings and facilities other assets of the university; corruption in related activities, including University Sport; branch corruption in to manage higher Teach, embezzlement, forgery and forgery, fraud, deliberately spreading misinformation about the quality and quantity of education nyh and related services; corruption in related industries and subdivisions activities, development and development, including the publication of textbooks, handbooks and monographs production and supply as well as the implementation of computer programs nyh materials, necessary for process learning.

Red flags (Red tape) - limitations, or simply

Used, or on purpose created officers for extraction personal benefits by To collect receive- flow. Any restrictions set by the relevant authorities can be seen as a red flag. Organizations cannot work ration without relating to licenses. universities immortality May to return diplomas Go-to indicate, to declare sample, immortality owner to indicate, to declare accreditation. Quantity licensed old and accredited Location also organized. Everything data limitations,How positive them immortality it seemed to want, to contribute development bribe.

Licensing - the process of granting the right to issue Services. Providing services without a suitable license, legal. Licensing is used by authorities to gain entry. Barriers to the education services market and "red flags" for aggregation bribe. Licensing can also be used for raider attacks curents. In this case, the license is canceled by government officials,serves as the basis for the closure of the organization and the transfer of its employees competitors.

Local monopoly - when characterizes the situation organization monopolizes the market for the provision of services in a particular area or in a particular area of expertise. As a result, prices rise. Extended The expansion of the service market and the increase in the mobility of market participants contribute to development. collapse local monopolies.

Low value or low quality goods (Low value goods) - may often found in the form of low-quality services sold in dumping your prices. A low value or low quality good is a demanded good. decreasing with growth Income.

scale corruption (Big corruption) - or corruption over- big characterizes corruption with high school middle size bribe or

embezzled funds. A typical example of large-scale corruption is bribery. entry to work. Large-scale embezzlement of funds and Tax avoidance moves are also large-scale corruption. With Other forms of large-scale corruption involve falsification of research. Telski grants medicine, as far as them accompaniment important they amount.

Petty corruption is a form of corruption, so small bribes and embezzlement of insignificant amounts of funds. A typical example of petty corruption is petty bribery and dark colors. Petty corruption is often confused with petty corruption. In fact, petty corruptions can reach the lion's share. because all corruption can be petty bribes, an important form of corruption and make up big part of all money source, received illegal path.

Dead Souls (Ghost staff) - faculty and other staff universities listed as full-time employees but not actually working shchih in given university and fail to fulfill responsibilities.

Monitoring _ format control level corruption in organizations. tracing provides regular and systemic To collect Information obtained from all possible sources or sources identified by Random sampling method to detect and evaluate corruption activity. The level of corruption is monitored through surveys and analysis. documents, comparison of facts, controls, reporting, confidential data telephone lines etc. Monitoring also aims to develop preventive measures. Effective strategy to fight corruption by detecting it at an early stage development. Monitoring can be done by the administration, the state. authorities, law enforcement, community groups, and nonprofits donor organizations.

Monopoly (Monopoly) - characterizes fully controlled organizations adjusting prices in local service markets or for specific special occasions handle. The monopoly position of individual authorities is fundamental. to eat for corruption.

monopsony (monopsonia) - Monopoly consumer.

Hired artists of academic work (Ghost writers) - or so So-called "Negroes" are professionals who do academic work. joyful order for money for customers.

ethics (violation of academic integrity) is characterized as: detects any form of behavior that violates officially established rules villa in organizations.

Breach intellectual ethic (Chewing related to intellectual integrity) -

breach Charter behaviour and activities in scientific community. Plagiarism and violation of research ethics are classic forms of violation. Answers intellectual ethics.

integrity , **any pro-**illegal behavior that violates officially established rules organizations.

illegal behaviour (Illegal behaviour) - characterizes none forms degenerate behaviour, forbidden live or Charter organizations.

Illegal tutoring (Unauthorized tutoring) - part- no private lesson, carried out in detour live.

unjustly good behaviour (Preferred treatment) - application giving undeserved priority to violating individuals established rules and professional and ethical standards. unfairly good Neck attitude characterizes a particular positive attitude based on gender. stva, friendship, personal sympathy and others distinguishing features.

uncontrollable corruption (uncontrolled corruption) - corruption, to find- beyond the effective control of government or organizations. uncontrollable hum corruption immortality a characteristic high school level corruption. Chalk- rock corruption over base levels maybe to stay uncontrollable in back then time as high school degenerate sector maybe function in fitwhwell-defined informal rules within a particular organizationrational buildings.

misappropriation - characterizes suspicious or misappropriation of the organization's funds. Incorrect allocation of resources has a negative impact on the development of the organization. reduction and her monetary location.

Uncertainty product (uncertainty related to output) - a basis corruption various spheres. Quality trainer Services, Researchand medical service complicated measurement.

Nepotism (Nepotism) - characterizes the very benevolent attitude management relatives, officers or other formal persons endowed with power forces.

unprofessional behaviour (Abuse) - characterizes none corrupt conduct prohibited by law or bylaws reduction.

Imperfect knowledge - characterizes what is not. The abundance of reliable information about the availability of services and prices for them in the corruption market national services. Organizations often intentionally hide their rights information customers, to the real prices of services, thus saving costs and increasing level profitability.

Evasion is the practice of hiding income to evade taxes. nonpayment taxes.

Unethical behavior characterizes any corruption. rational behavior in the organization. Corruption is an unethical behavior even if the organization does not have a formal code of conduct Denia.

Grassroots corruption (Street-level corruption) - characterizes corruption as: side employees and persons, directly Study with customers.

favors - characterizes the situation, when both parties abuse their positions, violate ethical standards we go beyond the legal framework, but enough to prove the fact of corruption difficult, because there is no exchange mediated by money. Both face-Crowns benefit from pleasant conversations and the costs are actually not small at all. day Pleasure exchange, typically a secret or secret corruption.

services (Logrolling) - according to the principle of "you to me, I to you" -rupee, also which? money immortality change they owners, them. immortality continues swapon money. The exchange of services is well suited to concealing corruption. Opposite Suitable swap continues also opposite confirmation side.

Oligarchy (Oligarchy) - characterizes the unification of the state and organization especially at the management level. The resulting relationships What happens from such a merger allows organizations to violate laws and regulations, evil to use trust societies Along with immunity.

Oligopoly (Oligopoly) - characterizes the position of close organizations monopoly. Limited number of employees and similar organizations, having the authority to take certain actions creates conditions of threat forming groups with common corrupt interests. oligopoly immortality provides separation functions between degenerate persons.

organizational structure bribe takers (Organizational structure related to contributors) - maybe hierarchical or horizontal.

Commission, share, commission (Payment) - a certain part or pro- cents to employees of the field who allocate government funds to a bidder to live in barter these funds bribe.

kickbacks (kickbacks) - bribe, mercenary after that commit behave degenerate-tion. May be required to receive government funds allocated to organizations Don't be afraid to bribe a government official who decides on your allocation .money source, a also timing allocation and dimensions financing. "Dead spirits",them. registered, however immortality Study, May interruption definite quantity from her wage fees Leader organizations or structural sections, partner second accepted to them over Work.

Money laundering is the process of legalizing money infected with viruses. nerdy illegal path. laundering from money most often meets in organizations partner important external financing.**Queuing** - or waiting -

characterizes the waiting time. gain access to limited resources. queues can form the basis for some types of corruption. Prejudice and a biased approach allocation of resources between organizations over time. tail disruption. Recipients of assets and funds bribe to expedite nia process promotion in queues and progressive they competitors.

package Services (Service packaging) - or at that time, What in your name "product in load" - application-tick binding mercenary Services one character with Services other with aim higher-nia reached organizations. Not anytime morally right.

patronage (Patronage) - or roofing, encase, auspices,

"umbrella" characterizes a system in which customers use certain information. privileges granted to them by their bosses. Such patronage or patronage leads to violations of the operating rules of organizations and is a kind of my corruption Patronage also happens when hiring and promoting individuals. climb the career ladder. Patronage violates merit-priority principles and weakens soul competition power.

Vote cheating - falsification of results Juggling voices of implicit voting is common in organizations. to manage i chose but not assigned.

Plutocracy is the power of money. the way to be high corrupt organizations Everything is bought and sold: jobs, diplomas, promotions, appointments, offices, business trips, financeelimination etc.

Fraud (Fraud) - falsification and deliberate misrepresentation. Forgery of documents, reviews, Research results and data.

Offer (Gift) - given with the expectation of receiving something illegally th, in return - a bribe. An offer made in the hope of getting something in return or illegal legally immortality a bribe in some countries.

gifts is a form of corruption. if this gift is a bouquet of flowers. Depending on the country and current situation offering a gift after the legislature has enjoyed an illegal advantage nym by immortality suitable for quality bribe.

positional meeting room capability (Bargain strength) - meeting roompower or negotiation power - the ability of each of those involved in the corruption to influence the other party in the negotiations of the parties. lesson corrupt negotiations are corrupt results. All information actions are based on positional and professional power. Location- Great negotiating ability of negotiators plays the role of foundation degenerate negotiations. Price:%s over degenerate Services, as rule we-

predetermined or determined transactions and procedures for the execution of transactionsalso defined.

positional capability extortion (usurper strength) - path- ness persons receive illegal fee by threats, blackmail and control above potential customers. Monopoly location, collusion formationcoalitions and hierarchical power are tools to strengthen positional relationships. affect with aim extortion bribe.

Political indoctrination (Political suggestion - political engage or politicize an organization or a particular issue, format violations Charter political impartiality and objectivity.

Receiver or recipient - the person receiving the bribe. All workers sectors render Services, buyers bribe, are buyers.

Corruption (corruption) - in narrow perception It means demolition evidence-evidence of corruption Corruption in a broad sense means the destruction of the core structure. goals, the purpose of the activity organizations.

format (Sequential organization) is a typical the form of organization of the corruption process in the activities of the organization naya. Receipt services definitely definite series.

Mediator - person acting as an intermediary in the discussion expect the possibility of bribery and transfer where they have agreed group, not individual. Political lobbyists representing interests government-level organizations broker. HORSE a little countries class mediation activities or lobbying a profession and requires special licenses.

Legal nihilism (Legal nihilism) - characterizes situation when? back-laws and regulations governing the scope of the organization are ignored. **neglect** (Neglect) - maybe evident organizations executive nitrates, a also to indicate, to declare authorities supervision. humiliating behaviour with patients in medical centers a more one format judicial neglect. neglect Charter and professional obya

busyness also a one from forms corruption.

persecution - implies any form persecution and sweeping on the side organizational leadership. distinguishing characteristic of the persecution of whistleblowers about violations in the organization, a fact of denunciation, but the fact that people inform state bodies of violations Decisions taken are not protected by law from administrative prosecutions. Reporting violations always involves risk, including the risk of losing Work, career growth and others potential opportunities.

White collar crime - that is. to serve It includes almost all corruption crimes in various forms. nyh fields, Like this as loyalty highly educated formal persons without applications violence. Term "Crimes "white collar" it happened first circulated at the annual conference of the American sociologist. Chess association in 1939. White collar crime defined divided as "a crime committed by a person with a good reputation" respect and high social status with the use of niem her formal provisions."

Coercion - is a typical characteristic factor associated with escort corruption. faces, occupation definite positions and domain power givers to scare potential customers extortion bribe. HORSE swap over support and cooperation, to indicate, to declare often ignores truths corruption in individual fields and participation in to them a little persons former them since, Goodbye level corruption immortality will begin threaten existence most over- lytic systems.

The double counting issue (Double counting issue) is an existing issue.schaya in dimension general Sound bribe, collected back definite period time- nor when the same amount of bribe is counted two or more times. for example, situation existence degenerate hierarchies quantities bribe distributed over vertical, from grass roots with top levels. Often special employees back Control transfer parts bribe to ensure yourself taking encase.

Market failures characterize the inadequacy of the market. mechanisms to ensure that services are delivered at a certain quality lazy time zone. Corruption fills the gaps left by the market or created parasitize states.

Sales affect (Interest peddlers) - characterizes employees and organic nations selling their influence in exchange for bribes. government officials offer licensing and accreditation in swap over bribe. doctors offer pharmaceutical campaigns summer patients definitely to them medicines in swap over Stock these campaigns or Share in snow.

Sale of authority (Influence trading) - or authorization trading - mi characterizes the informal practice of commerce for the exchange of services. violation of the code of conduct established by the organization. full sale abuse of office and format corruption.

corruption in various fields **(immediate**

costs) listed as total all mercenary bribe.

Balance bribes - resulting bribes balancing the supply and demand of corrupt services. Balance- bribery is essentially the market price of corrupt services in this case. ioli another field.

Waste source of money (Gross waste) - characterizes untargeted and insufficient use source of money. Waste money source, continuing

it can be considered a form of corruption deliberately and for personal gain. tion. The costs of an organization's ancillary activities are an example of waste. bury source of money.

Racism is the practice of corrupt discrimination based on: and racial identity. Racism is banned in many countries, but still he is develops in hidden forms.

embezzlement, embezzlement, embezzlement - to characterize Illegal use of budget funds, income and property is prohibited. for personal purposes, unlawfully and to the detriment of the enterprise or organization zation

Door keeping is an access control application . wounded resources.

Spoil (spoil) - This active phase unfriendly takeovers businessesor her assets.

raider (raid) - participant forward takeovers or forward attacks.

Raiding is the hostile takeover of a business or other assets. tivov, representative value over market, to express process to fight backdistribution and redistribution of property using corruption and official forgery. At a functional level, it is possible to raidIn a system where there are loopholes in the legislation. Customization before- nationalized systems and businesses maybe also Used for raid.

Sales suggestions (Sales suggestions) - a form of corruption that the authorities refused to give information to the applicants persons Suggestions, is necessary in others organizations.

behavior is typical corrupt behavior Corrupt officials and bureaucrats Obtaining personal benefit from official duties without applying special efforts. Monopoly position in terms of control over access worthless resources allows to collect rent in format bribe.

risk - probability of encountering a correction corruption in the organisation. The risk of corruption is closely related to blackmail and blackmail. necessity to give bribe.

risk - possibility of corruption not to be discovered, disclosed, accused of corruption or convicted tion. The risk of a corrupt official depends on the effectiveness of the fight against corruption. on behalf of the administration and law enforcement. If leadership and law enforcement ignores, encourages, or directly natural participation in corruption, The risk of corruption is low.

Collusion is a typical form of corruption. collusion Location in situation, when? participants corruption finalize agreement for far-

most common activities. For this reason, colleagues often ignore corruption. behaviour they acquaintances and cover to them.

Covert corruption - includes forms of corruption cases where there is no money exchange bribe. Nepotism, arrogance, and nice words are classic forms of behavior. mi hidden corruption.

Hidden fees - hidden expenses baths in packages. Overly and unfairly expensive accommodation dormitories, clearly inflated tariffs for other services, etc. classical Russian forms of corruption. The data of the form is deliberately based. deliberately providing incomplete or incorrect information about the quality and prices of services over to them.

Justice (Impartiality) - principle ethic behaviour, over basis partner tori employees be interested with everybody customers in equal degree well, in corresponding stvii with requirements, established in organizations, and laws countries.

Average bribe amount - average bribe paid calculated as the weighted average of the total in a given year the number of corrupt bribes received by buyers and the total numbers bribe.

Incentives (Incentives) - degenerate

behaviour - This reasons, over cat- eye subjects of various fields of activity, managers, administrators, workers, to indicate, to declare and business violate laws and set of rules with aim arrangement and make sure productive activities these spheres. Incentives often expressed as tangible and intangible benefits received or promised participants degenerate transactions.

guard gatekeepers, guard (Door Keepers) - role employees and administrations regulating access to limited intangible assets resources, and bestowed live vote.

Gas pedal (Grease money) - accelerator bribe or "grease" To let- overcome the bureaucracy obstacles, neutralize dissonance the laws of the shenstvo or their backwardness and inconsistency with the spirit of the times, and also rooting positive decision-making processes. Rule "sub- The principle of "self" and "If you do not lubricate, you will not go" are well known. bureaucrats may deliberately create bureaucratic obstacles for personal gain by demanding accelerator bribes. Such bribes are paid sometimes to government officials to take over the management of organizations all kinds permissions, in Sound including licenses and accreditations.

falsification diplomas (Diploma dishonest) - fake documents about Education provided by accredited universities. Unlike factories, diplomatic mov is a fake that produces its own unsupported diplomas. sifters diplomas to beat trainer documents well dawn-established state and foundation universities, as a rule, accreditation. Diplomas of these universities are in demand in the labor market. they are allowed to hold certain positions and are recognized by the state. wrong certification of diplomas depending on the legislation of a particular country is an infringement of trademark, copyright or intellectual property rights Noah Real estate.

Fictitious (listed) teachers (Ghost trainers) - or dead - your souls are teachers registered to the department and/or infected bot wages, even though they don't teach and don't practice scientific, methodical or other real work. fake teachers tel, registered with the department, share the fees received with the management dstvom, which registers them in the state. Other teachers value non-wagenot wages, but the position on the pulpit, because it brings them other profits, including career advancement. In return, they provide Professional quality services to customers at discounted prices Price:%s or free. With categories lots kind "teachers" lawyers, certified accountants and auditors, bankers, doctors and others experts. Other categories of fictitious persons are employees of local institutions. Officials benefiting from university lecturer status, as well as providing employers with certain preferences in return same encase to them for small violations of the law.

Predator - employee of a corrupt organization it moves regularly and, above all, takes into account its position. as a source of corruption proceeds, neglecting the authorities responsibilities. wild animal - corrupt professional. HE IS interested in more potential bribery. Hunters often try receive external financing with aim her next assignments.

messenger or petitioner is an employee who addresses a person. novnik with to request to make a decision he is or different question back money her apprentice.

Private tutoring is the practice of giving private lessons. lovemaking services in private, if not it's normal banned by law.

save over scale (Economy related to scale) - in corruption reached if they cooperate and negotiate with an employee about the size of Bribes as a group, not individually. A single bribe collected by the group for all participants maybe get smaller over size, How integrity all bribe, data individually.

Forwarder (Accelerator) - a person who performs negotiation functions with to speed up and facilitate the bureaucratic decision-making process. for the benefit of the customer. The agent or forwarder does not make any personal connections so you, information peoples, systems and mechanisms processing documents and information-Uses legal loopholes, loopholes and professional connections, persuading officials of the safety of a corrupt deal and mutual benefit. Lobbyists represent organizations in the acquisition process. government financing, business leaders bargain licenses and accreditation also to indicate, to declare organizations.

flexibility is an indicator of susceptibility reluctance of the authorities to change the level and nature of the proposal bribe potential customers.

Elasticity of demand - a measure of sensitivity potential bribes or donors with change Price:%s over degenerate we-meadows. Under Price:%s implied size is necessary bribe.

EPISODE one. GENERAL REGULATIONS

Article 1. Basic terms and definitions used in this Law The following basic terms and their definitions are used in this Law: **corruption** - deliberate, deliberate, planned use public formal or

a foreign official of his or her equivalent illegal semi-related position and related opportunities, property or other in the form of a service, patronage, pre-commitment Bribery of a public official as well as property for himself or a third party by a person or an equivalent person or a foreign official providing property to them or another benefits in format Services, auspices, by promising benefits to themselves or to third partiesan official or an equivalent person or a foreign official undertakes or refrains from doing their official duties; nyh (labor) responsibilities;

state officials - President of the Republic of Belarus, deputies tattoos rooms representatives, members Council Republic National meetings Res-

The Belarusian people, deputies of the local House of Representatives, fulfill their duties. powers on a professional basis alongside other civil servants subject to the state legislation of the Republic of Belarus civil service (hereinafter referred to as civil servants); Investigative Committee staff Committee of the Republic of Belarus with special ranks (hereinafter referred to as Follow-up employees) State Committee of the Republic of Belarus); persons, permanently or temporarily or privately serving in the Armed Forces of the Republic Belarus, other troops and military formations, bodies of the Republic of Belarus internal affairs, emergency bodies and departments, financial Financial investigations of the State Control Committee of the Republic of Belarus and In accordance with the legislative acts of the Republic of Belarus, the relevant officials (hereinafter referred to as military personnel, special and command personnel) internal affairs bodies, bodies and units for emergencies, organization New financial investigations of the State Control Committee of the I Republic larus); persons occupied permanently or temporarily or by a special authority positions related to the performance of organizational and administrative or administrative staff ministries and economic duties in government organizations and non-governmental organizations state organizations in which the share of state ownership is in the authorized capital not veins little 50 percent;

persons equivalent to public officials (equivalent relevant persons) , - Members of the National Assembly of the Republic of the Republic Belarus, deputies of local Councils of Representatives exercising their powers non-professional basis; legally registered citizens Candidates for the President of the Republic of Belarus, candidates for parliament most representatives, members of the National Assembly of the Republic, the Council of the Republic Belarus, deputies of the local House of

Representatives; persons, permanently or temporarily, or special powers occupying positions in non-state organizations Economic duties related to the implementation of corporate and administrative or administrative practices, but excluding the persons specified in the <u>third paragraph</u> standing article; persons fully authorized to take legal action mentally significant actions; people in the performance of their duties. protection of public order, fight against crime, administration justice;

foreign formal faces - formal faces foreign to indicate, to declare charities, members of foreign public assemblies, international organizations, international parliamentary councilors, judges and officials faces International the courts;

property - immovable and movable things (including money and securities) gi), including property rights established by civil lawRepublic of Belarus;

close relatives - parents, children, adoptive parent accepted (Ah-

rennie), local Siblings and sisters, Grandfather, Grandmother, grandchildren;

family members - husband (wife), close relatives living together stno and leading general household with a civil servant or equalwith he is face;

mother-in-laws - close relatives spouse (wives);

conflict of interest - personal interests of the state officer, spouse (spouse), close relatives, or father- in-law who influence or may affect the appropriate performance of public officials face they formal (labor) responsibilities also acceptance to them Answers or participation in acceptance Answers or commit others action over service (Work).

Matter 2nd. Legislation about to fight with corruption

based on the constitution Republican- It contains the faces of Belarus and this Law and other legislative acts of the Republic. folk Belarus, a also International treaties Republic Belarus.

Responsibility for crimes that create the conditions for corruption, and Corruption crimes <u>are determined by law</u> Advertisement about the Republic of Belarus- ministry crimes, penal <u>code</u> Republic of Belarus and other legislative actions Republic of Belarus.

Article 3corruption crimes

The subjects of the crimes that constitute the conditions of corruption are as follows: to indicate, to declare formal faces;

persons are equal to public servants.The subjects of corruption crimes are as follows: to indicate, to declare formal faces;

persons equivalent to public officials; foreign formal faces;

face, to apply bribe to indicate, to declare formal or equalnyh with he is persons or foreign formal persons.

Matter 4. principles to fight with corruption

to fight with corruption based over principles:

legality; justice; equality former by law; promotion;

the inevitability of responsibility; personal guilt;humanism.

Matter 5. system quantity to fight with corruption

The fight against corruption is carried out by state bodies and other organizations. through organizations inclusive implementation of the following quantity:

Planning and coordination of activities of government agencies and other organizations organizations wrestle with corruption;

identification of special requirements as well as restrictions financial control over public officials purposes prevention manifestations corruption and them identification;

ensure the legal regulation of the activities of state bodies, and other organizations, state and public supervision and control of this activity force;

improvement of the system of state bodies, personnel work and procedures for resolving problems that ensure the protection of rights, freedoms and legitimate interests physically and legal persons;

To carry out activities aimed at informing the public, to contribute to the formation of society, creating an atmosphere of intolerance towards corruption (anti-corruption training english and growing);

make sure promotion in activities to indicate, to declare formal and equal nyh with he is persons, if other immortality provided legislation Republic Belarus;

restoration of violated rights, freedoms and legitimate interests of individuals and legal persons, elimination of other harmful consequences of crimes, shchih conditions for corruption and degenerate crimes;

impose legal prohibitions to distinguish between civil servants (labor) State duties and personal, group and other non-duty interests formal and equal with he is persons;

provision in accordance with the legislative acts of the Republic of Belarus guarantees to government officials and persons equal to them, and compensation related with limitations established hereby live and other legislative actions Republic Belarus in the field to fight with corruption;

prevent funding or provide other types of material Sourcing the activities of government agencies and other organizations from resources and OK, immortality envisaged legislation Republic of Belarus;

to carry out criminological examination of the projects in accordance with the established procedure Legislative acts of the Republic of Belarus, previously adopted (published) legal acts Criminological studies of the Belarusian people and corruption crimes to assess and predict to identify the preconditions and causes of corruption, and on time acceptance effective measures over he is warning and prevention;

combining the fight against corruption with the creation of economic prerequisites eliminate reasons corruption.

EPISODE 2nd

FIGHTING STATE POWERS

CORRUPTION AND SPECIAL UNIT. GOVERNMENT AUTHORITIES AND OTHER INSTITUTIONS ATTENDED HORSE FIGHTING WITH CORRUPTION

Matter 6. to indicate, to declare bodies, to apply to fight with corruption

The fight against corruption is carried out by the prosecutor's office, internal affairs and state bodies. State security.

State bodies involved in the fight against corruption, tasks that they face independently and in interaction with each other and with others with the help of state bodies and other organizations, as well as citizens Republic of Belarus.

Matter 7. forces General prosecution Republic Belarus in sphere to fight with corruption

General prosecution Republic Belarus a public establishment name, responsible back fighting organization with corruption.

HORSE purposes make sure organizations to fight with corruption General prosecutionra Republic Belarus:

collects information about facts that testify to corruption; analyzes the effectiveness of the anti-corruption measures implemented; coordinates law enforcement activity other to indicate, to declare establishment

new, to apply to fight with corruption;

supervises the execution by the heads of state bodies and other organizations fulfill the requirements of this Law and other legal acts of the Republic.Public Belarus in the field of anti-corruption and in the case of detection of crimes takes measures to hold those who commit themselves to account, lazy legislative actions Republic of Belarus;

prepares proposals for the improvement of the legal regulation of the struggle. corruption;

exercise other powers in the field of anti-corruption established by legislative acts Republic Belarus.

Matter eight. Special sections over to fight with corruption and to them Rights

In the prosecutor's office, internal affairs

and state security organs, has special combat units with corruption.

The procedure for its creation in the prosecutor's office, internal affairs and state bodies The security of the special anti-corruption units is determined by the Front Management. resident Republic Belarus.

Special units for the fight against corruption in the performance of duties ladies over tasks are entitled to:

receive free of charge from government bodies and other organizations in the charter Updated legislation of the Republic of Belarus, necessary information to perform anti-corruption functions, including automated ones. bathrooms information, reference systems and banks data;

Arriving freely at state border checkpoints the territory of the Republic of Belarus and places where border control is carried out, black certificates and passes, issuance to indicate, to declare anger Authorized officials of the Committee of the Republic of Belarus or other organizations sizes anger Services Republic of Belarus;

suspension, in whole or in part, with the sanction of the prosecutor, until the end ten-day financial transactions of natural and legal persons, as well as limited Give them the right to dispose of the property if there is sufficient reason to do so. assuming that funds and (or) other property are received from persons involved commission of corruption crimes or legalization of received income judicial by;

bring in to indicate, to declare sizes and other to indicate, to declare organizations in OK,established legislation Republic Belarus, representation about cancel special permissions (licenses) over application individual Species activities.

Among other rights, the protection of special unitsCorruption is determined by this Law and other legal acts of the Republic. folk Belarus.*Article 9. State organs and other organizations participating in the warwith corruption*

Investigative Committee of the Republic of Belarus, State Con- Control of the Republic of Belarus and its bodies, State Customs Committee of the Republic of Belarus Belarusian people and customs of the

Republic of Belarus, State Border Committee of the Republic of Belarus and other bodies of the border service of the Republic of Belarus, Ministry of Taxes and Charges of the Republic of Belarus and its inspections, Minister Finance and regional bodies of the Republic of Belarus, National Bank of the Republic of Belarus, other banks and non-bank financial institutions and other government agencies and other organizations are participating in the struggle against it. Corruption within its authority in accordance with the legislation of the Republic of folk Belarus.

Article 10. Interaction of government agencies and other organizations sphere fight against corruption

State organs and other organizations are obliged to transfer the state. anti-corruption officials, information about the incident full, testimony about corruption.

Procedure and conditions for interaction carried out by state bodies to fight with corruption is determined by them together.

State bodies involved in the fight against corruption, International agreements of the Republic of Belarus can exchange necessary information formation with authorities foreign states, to apply activity in sphere to fight with corruption.

Article 11 corruption, government bodies and other organizations involved in the fight against corruptioncorruption

State bodies, other organizations and their officials In addition to its powers, citizens of the Republic of Belarus are also obliged to provide assistance. state bodies and state bodies involved in the fight against corruption military authorities and other organizations involved in the fight against corruption. Intelligence, Documents and other materials in the field of anti-corruption requested by the government government bodies that fight corruption are given to the government donors, other organizations and their officials immediately literally, a if This impossible then in flow three days.

information and documents involving government, bankingor other protected live a secret carried out in OK, envisaged legalto give Republic Belarus. Providing specified information and documents wasp- It is possible in terms, envisaged Section first real article.

Matter 12. informative security to fight with corruption

To collect, store, analyze and summarize information about facts, witnesses corruption, including individuals and legal entities involved corruption creates and maintains special anti-corruption units xia operational accounting and centralized banks data.

The Prosecutor General's Office of the Republic of Belarus maintains unified data banks about ingenious to fight with corruption which? created over basis information,

represented by the prosecution, home affairs and state security sti in the manner and on the terms established by the Prosecutor General's Office of the Republic of BelarusIn agreement with the Ministry of Internal Affairs of the Republic of Belarus and the Committee state security Republic of Belarus.

Article 13those involved in the fight against corruption and relevant government agencies and other organizationsin to fight with corruption

coordination of the activities of state bodies involved in the fight against government bodies and other organizations involved in the fight against corruption It is carried out by coordinating meetings to fight corruption and crime. Corruption and corruption acting as determined by the President Belarus.

Article 14sections wrestle with corruption

Financial and logistical support of special subdivisions anti-corruption measures are carried out at the expense of the republican budget he is. The specific amount of funds (including foreign exchange) required for this, properly established when approving the republican budget for maintenance organs of the prosecution, internal affairs and state security and are usedthem logistics provision of special units.

EPISODE 3

A WARNING CORRUPTION

Article 15bodies in the economic field and other government organizationswearing

Solutions for providing state support to legal entities and Individual entrepreneurs are accepted as determined by the President. Republic of Belarus.

As prescribed by government bodies and other government organizations renovated legislation Republic Belarus, compulsory to manage open competitions or auctions also acceptance Answers:

legal entities and (or) individual entrepreneurs public application programs and to indicate, to declare orders;

about allocation of quotas;

about vote suppliers for to indicate, to declare needs;

on imposing on a legal entity and (or) an individual entrepreneur individual functions government client;

In other cases provided for by the legislation of the Republic of Belarus. Method and order distribution quotas over external Trade goods to identify

It is made by the President of the Republic

of Belarus or by the Government of the Republic of Belarus on his behalf. folk Belarus.

Open auctions and auctions to distribute quotas and select materials boxes for government needs are not made if there are relevant consumables. vars (Works, Services) carried out organization, structure natural mono-

police, also in cases permitted by the legislation of the Republic of Belarus-xia different order distribution quotas and vote suppliers for state needs.

Article 16 be interested in over class positions to indicate, to declare formal faces

public official, person applying for office public official to prevent possible actions lead to the use of official positions and associated consequences. opportunities and empowerment based on personal, group and other off-duty situations interests give an obligation to comply with the restrictions set by Art.17 of this Law and state legislation of the Republic of Belarusmilitary service for civil servants (if the relevant position is public servant means public service) and about fame legal consequences of not complying lots obligations.

Obligation of a public official, a person making an application The occupation of the position of a public official shall be regulated in writing. personnel service of the relevant state body, form of other organization tion. Failure to sign this obligation entails refusing to register. as a candidate for a public official position, appointed the position of a public official or the release of a public official officer from office as prescribed by the legislature no moves Republic Belarus.

Personnel service officials of the relevant government agency to another organization for not fulfilling its official duties.over record obligations to indicate, to declare formal face, face, allegation-blowing or untimely to occupy the position of a public official replaceable familiarity to indicate, to declare formal persons with presented with he is requirements carry disciplinary responsibility as prescribed by law legislative acts Republic Belarus.

Article 17. Restrictions on public officials and equal against them to indicate, to declare formal face immortality Right:engage in commercial activities personally or through trusted persons persons, spouse, close relatives or nicknames in the implementation of entrepreneurial activities using the picture Being the representative of third parties in matters related to the position, activities government body, other organization, having an employee (employee) (which herd) either dependent (sub) and (or) controlled (sub) control) to him (his) state body, other organization, and also to carry out other paid work not related to the performance of official (work) obligations main service (work) employment (teaching, scientific, cultural, creative activity and medical practice), unless otherwise stated leno constitution Republic Belarus;

Making commitments on behalf of government agencies without the consent of the government state bodies (organizations) to which they are subject (behavior) (in to connect which? them including), opportunities with legal persons owners immu-

company or its affiliates in accordance with the legislation The actions of the

Republic of Belarus on commercial companies are peer ha), close relatives or father-in-laws and individual entrepreneurs spouse, close relative or as well as partners to entrust the execution of these transactions without such consent otherwise formal persons;

on behalf of non-governmental organizations with registered capitalshare of state property at least 50 percent, legal proceedings private persons, property owners or dependents In accordance with the economic legislative acts of the Republic of Belarus associations are spouses, close relatives or father-in-laws, and also with individual entrepreneurs who have spouses, entrusting such commissions, as well as close relatives or father-in-laws actions against other officials violating the procedure established by the legislature no moves Republic of Belarus economic societies;

take part in business management personally or through trusted persons Except for the cases stipulated in this Law, the organization and other legislature actions of the republic Belarus;

have accounts in foreign banks, excluding

government lawsuits Gift functions in foreign states and in other cases established by legislative acts Republic Belarus;

follow instructions on official (labor) activities and the instructions of a political party or other public association that is a member (who) he (excluding deputies and members of the House of Representatives) Council of the National Assembly of the Republic of Belarus, local deputies soviets MPs).

Republic of Belarus for civil servants, as well as employees of the Investigative Committee of the Republic of Belarus, military personnel, persons Special and boss composition sizes internal works, sizes and sections over emergencies, financial investigative bodies of the State Committee control Republic Belarus May to be Established other limitations.

Civil servants and employees of the Republican Investigation Committee Belarusian people, military personnel, privates and commanders of the organization new internal affairs bodies and departments, bodies for emergencies monetary investigations Board to indicate, to declare control Republic darned-

Russia, to have participation shares (shares, rights) in the authorized funds of the company business organizations, within three months from the date of appointment (election) to transfer to the trust management under the guarantee of the state for a while civil service, service on the Republican Investigation Committee Military service (service) in the Armed Forces of the Republic of Belarus, other other troops and military formations of the Republic of Belarus, internal affairs bodies, bodies and departments for emergencies, financial investigative bodies Board to indicate, to declare control Republic of Belarus.

Government officials not mentioned in the third part of this section article, owner in Real estate shares participation (Stock, Rights) in legal source of money Contact

commercial organizations have the right to participate in person or through authorized persons. manage them commercial establishments.

A public official is obliged to suspend his membership. political party, if in accordance with the legislation of the Republic of Belarus, performance of state functions is incompatible belonging political party.

A public official who violates a written obligation compliance with the restrictions set by the first, third and fifth parts of this article related articles liability, including the release busy positions, in OK, established legislative actions Republic Belarus.

Restrictions on persons considered public servants, established legislative acts Republic of Belarus.

Article 18 organizations spouses, relatives relatives or mother-in-laws

Restrictions on the joint civil service of civil servants Joint service of employees of the Investigative Committee of the Republic of Belarus, military personnel, private and commanding personnel of internal affairs bodies, bodies and departments for emergencies, financial investigative bodies Joint work of the State Control Committee of the Republic of Belarus same state organization of other persons (separate subdivision), with spouses, close relatives or father-in-laws, resident vayutsya legislative actions of the republic Belarus.

Article 18 [1]. Procedure for preventing and resolving conflicts of interestLinks with to apply responsibilities to indicate, to declare formal faces

to indicate, to declare formal face compulsory inform in written format about the leader, to whom he is directly attached, The emergence or possibility of a conflict of interest should be addressed as soon as possible. realizes this and has the right to declare in writing that it withdraws from acceptance. make a decision, participate in a decision, or take other action service (business) that causes or may cause a conflict of interest owls The President may not accept the declared public official. withdraw himself and compel the public official to make a written commitment appropriate actions for the service (business). about the occurrence or possibility no conflict of interest and the results of the assessment of the declared state self-retraction by a military official informs head-on to indicate, to declare body, other organizations.

Head of a government body, which

becomes another organization being aware of the occurrence or possibility of a conflict of interest, now take precautions over her prevention or settlement.

Management to prevent or resolve conflicts of interest, phone government agency, other organization Right:

providing written advice on adoption to a public official ti precautions over prevention or conflict resolution areas of interest;to pick up to indicate, to declare formal face from commit action over service (business), which causes or may cause a public official faces conflict areas of interest;

transfer a public official as prescribed by law The Government of the Republic of Belarus, from a position, for the performance of tasks caused or may cause a conflict of interest, on the other hand important location;

teach yield former formal responsibilities over new Study place ortargetredfieldtesdapit official , including temporaryPrivate person in accordance with the procedure established by the legislation of the Republic of Belarus , prevention conflict areas of interest or opportunities her formation;

To take other measures provided for by the legislation of the Republic of Belarus. to indicate, to declare formal face, leader in directly subordinate

sti to who HE IS located, supervisor to indicate, to declare body, different organizations, former- Thoewho violate the conditions stipulated in this article will be liable. ness in fit with legislative actions Republic Belarus.

The requirements provided by this article do not apply to contributors. stnikov relationships, organized legislative actions Republic Belarus, establishment of penal order, administrative process, constitutional foot, civilian legal process legal process in economic courts

Matter nineteen. Quantity, directed over security monetary control

Government officials and their equivalents, their spouse (spouse) and prominent adult close relatives living with them entry of citizens of the Republic of Belarus into the state, as well as the common economy gift service, service in the Investigative Committee of the Republic of Belarus, military service under a contract, service in internal affairs bodies, organs and departments Emergencies, financial investigative bodies of the State Committee State control of the Republic of Belarus is mandatory in the prescribed cases and in the manner. Legal acts of the Republic of Belarus, declarations of income and Real estate appropriate government agency (organization).

Failure to declare income and assets or intentional contributions Incomplete, incorrect information is grounds for refusing to be accepted. service (job), reassignment or discipline responsibility, including dismissal rowing, established legislative actions of the republic Belarus.

Information contained in income and property declarations, distribution, except for cases stipulated by legal regulations - Is it a republic? Belarus.

Article 20. Offenses constituting the conditions of corruption The crimes constituting the conditions of corruption are: intervene to indicate, to declare formal faces with using they

official powers in the activities of other government agencies and other organizations is not within their jurisdiction and is not based on legislation, behave Republic Belarus;

provision provided by a public official in the preparation and adoption of decisions unlawful preference for the interests of individuals or legal entities granting them unreasonable benefits or privileges, or their provision;

use by a public official or equivalentformal provisions also decision Questions affecting her personal, groupand the other off duty areas of interest, if This immortality related partner formal activity;

involvement of a public official as a third-party attorney Persons who are in the business of the organization for which they serve or are subordinate or subordinate check it out different organizations;

use public formal or equal with he is face in personal, group and other informal interests involving information , commercial, banking or other protectedlive a secret received also to apply to them formal (labor) responsibilities;

refusal by a public official or equivalent person to provide providing information to individuals or legal entities, their provision these persons are provided for by the legislation of the Republic of Belarus, unintentionally timely provision or incomplete or incorrect provision information;

the request of a public official or an equivalent person natural or legal persons of the information, including the documents provided girl which is not provided legislation Republic Belarus;

by a public official, personal, group and other Non-commissioned interests created by the legal acts of the Republic of Belarus Russian of the procedure for considering and accepting applications from individuals or legal entities decisions about problems in in his competence;

a public official or an equivalent person,viv physically or legal persons in application to them Right and legitimate areas of interest;

delegation forces over to indicate, to declare arrangement entrepreneur- being controlled by the activity or the person carrying out that activity validity, if This immortality provided legislative actions Republic Belarus;

Violation of the tender and auction arrangement procedure determined by law to give Republic Belarus;

obligation to provide gratuitous (sponsored) assistance, and Violation of the procedure for the provision and use established by law vomit Republic Belarus.

commit specified in parts first real article crimes includes backyourself responsibility in fit with legislative actions Republic Belarus.

EPISODE 4

CORRUPTION CRIMES

Matter 21. Degenerate crimes

Degenerate crimes are:

extortion public formal or equal with he is face or foreign formal face Real estate or another benefits in format Services, over-

auspices, promises Benefits for myself or for third persons in swap over none dei-action or inactivity also to apply formal (labor) responsibilities;

accepted by a public official or an equivalent person, or by another official in the form of a foreign property or service, a promise of benefit for oneself or third parties in exchange for something action or inaction in the performance of official (business) duties, except provided by law Republic of Belarus payment labor;

offer or grant to a public official or equivalent the person assigned to it or a foreign property or other official benefits in format Services, auspices, promises Benefits for to them or for third parties in exchange for any act or omission in the performance of official duties (labor) responsibilities;

action or inaction of a public official or equivalent person or a foreign official in official (worker) performance vyh) obligations for the purpose of obtaining an unlawful benefit in the form of a service, evidence, promises of advantage for yourself or for third persons;

illegal use or deliberate concealment of property taken a public official or an equivalent person or a foreigner officer from any activity specified in paragraphs two, three and three fifth parts first real article;

accepted by a public official or an equivalent person, or foreign formal face Real estate (Gifts) or another benefits in format Services in connection with the performance of official (labor) duties, with the exception of souvenirs , considered worthy also to apply protocol and other formal Events;

acceptance of an invitation from a public official or similar a tourist, health-improving, or a person embarking on another trip at the expense of physical harm legal and (or) legal persons, with the exception of the following trips: by invitation niyu spouse (wife), close relatives or mother-in-laws; was carried out in in accordance with international agreements of the Republic of Belarus or mutually on the basis of agreement between state bodies of the Republic of Belarus and foreign state bodies at the expense of the funds of the relevant state government bodies and (or) international organizations; at the invitation of other peoplelegal entities, if relations with them do not affect the subjects of their official (labor) activities the determination of the invitee; carried out with the approval of a higher authority person or colleague governing body to participate in international and foreign events conduct scientific, sports, creative and other activities at public expense associations (foundations), including excursions within the framework of the legal activities of such public associations (foundations) by invitation andControl foreign partners;

transfer by a public official to individuals as well as informal persons government agencies budget funds or other property found state ownership unless prescribed by the legislature actions of the republic Belarus;

individual, group and other off duty areas of interest privileged he is for application to indicate, to declare functions of state ownership, if any immortality provided legislative acts Republic of Belarus;

exercise of official powers by a public official loans, loans, securities purchases, real estate and other Real estate.

commit specified in parts first real article crimes includes backyourself responsibility in fit with legislative actions Republic Belarus.

Article 22. Notification of conditional offensefor corruption or corruption crimes

If any of the specified in the section is committed articles 20 and parts By the deputy of the House of Representatives of the first article of the 21st article of this Law. Lei, member of the Council of the National Assembly of the Republic of Belarus, deputies tatom of the local Council of Deputies, registered to a resident citizen as a candidate for the President of the Republic of Belarus according to the law, as a nominee Members of the House of Representatives, the National Assembly of the Republic, the Council of the Republic public Belarus, deputies local soviets deputies, to indicate, to declare bodies, While executing the fight against corruption, it notifies the Chamber accordingly. Council of Representatives, National Assembly of the Republic of Belarus, relating to local House of Representatives, vote commission.

Matter 23. Guarantee physically persons convenient Diagnostics corruption

A person reporting a corruption-related crime or otherwise contributes to the detection of corruption, is protected states.

A person who has contributed to the detection of corruption, his spouse (support friend), close relative or relatives in the presence of sufficient data, stating that there was a real threat of murder against them, using violence, destruction or damage to property, other illegal acts, implementation of security measures OK, established legislation Republic Belarus.

EPISODE 5

ELIMINATION RESULTS CORRUPTION CRIMES

Article 24bridges provided illegally Services

Funds provided in violation of the laws of the Republic of which was taken from the bank account of Belarus and a government official, or a person equal to him is subject to transfer by himself to the republican budget. public official or equivalent does it with he is face it was about known.

Goods, including gifts received by a public official or a person equal to himself by violating the procedure established by law Legal acts of the Republic of Belarus on the execution of official acts (labor) taxes are subject to free delivery at the service (work) place specified person. Accounting, storage, valuation and sale of the delivered property lyayutsya in as prescribed legislative acts Republic of Belarus.

If it is not possible to return the property and deliver it at the place of service (work) a public official or an equivalent person is obliged to pay him compensation. to pay back the cost of services, as well as the cost of services, into the republican budget he took advantage of it illegally by transferring money to the republic lycan budget in OK, established legislation Republic Belarus.

Family members of a public official or an

equivalent person,It has the right to accept property and services, including tourist invitations. health promotion and other excursions at the expense of individuals and legal entities located in live in official or other dependence on that government official or equal him face, associated with her officer (labor) activity.

A public official or an equivalent person must pass a non-mandatory examination. property taken by family members to the financial authority where it is legally locatedresidence or reimbursement of the cost or cost of non-entitled services Members of his family benefited from this by transferring funds. Public budget in the manner prescribed by the legislation of the Republic of Belarus Russian. Funds provided in violation of the legislation of the Republic Received from the bank account of family members of Belarus and the state private or equivalent person, transferable to the republic public official or equal with he is face it was about known.

In case of assignment of a public official or an equivalent person appears to be voluntarily surrendering property illegally acquired by him or his family members to reimburse the property or the cost of services or services received illegally or members of his family, this property or The corresponding service cost is subject to collection in government revenue on the following basis:decision of the court on the claim of state bodies fighting against illegality rupee. State bodies involved in the fight against corruption, before contacting the court has the right to confiscate property illegally obtained by the state. an official or equivalent person or a foreign official face, immortality have diplomatic immunity.

Property acquired by a government body or other government organization that violates the financing procedure, by the competent state bodies or court decision and its sequential implementation Established for the sale of property in accordance with the legislation of the Republic of Belarus, service fees that are confiscated, arrested or converted into government revenue, from breach How are you today? order, - numbering in republican budget.

Article 25 festival, create conditions for corruption, or degenerate crimes

Decisions taken as a result of the commission of circumstantial crimes Can be revoked by the state for corruption or corruption crimes by a donor organization, other organization or authorized officialor a higher state body, for their acceptance by another higher authority. an organization, a senior official, or a court in state action bodies, other organizations or citizens Republic Belarus.

Natural or legal person with rights and legally protected interests disadvantageous in conclusion acceptance lots Answers titled attractive to them in judicial OK.

Article 26 crimes create conditions for corruption, or degenerate crimes

Damage, caused commit crimes create conditions for corruption or the crime of corruption is compensated according to the procedure established by name legislative actions Republic Belarus.

By requirements, related with pay back damage caused commit Good-a crime that creates the conditions for corruption or a crime of corruption ,Established ten year old term allegation prescriptions, countable partner days to them commission.

Article 27. Duties and Responsibilities of Heads of State bodies, other for organizations refusal quantity over to fight with corruption

Heads of government agencies and other organizations within them Required for qualifications:

To accept the legislation created by this Law and other legal regulations WA Republic belarusian measures, directed over to fight with corruption;

It includes persons who commit crimes that create conditions for corruption offenses involving corruption or discipline national liability to such liability as prescribed by law. legal process Republic Belarus;

Informing on time in accordance with the legislation of the Republic Belarus, in order of state bodies involved in the fight against corruption, facts of crime by subordinates creating conditions for corruption or corruption crimes.

Heads of government agencies and other

organizations that do not comply or does not fully comply with the requirements set out in the first part of the Agreement. In addition to this article, those who do not provide the information requested by the state involved in the fight against corruption and necessary While performing their duties, they bear responsibility in accordance with the legislation. Is it a republic? Belarus.

EPISODE 6

CONTROL And SUPERVISION BACK ACTIVITIES OVER to fight With CORRUPTION

Article 28. Control over the activities of special combat unitswith corruption

Control over the activities of special units for the fight against corruption Ghana handles the prosecution, internal affairs and state security related proceedings. substantially General Prosecutor Republic Belarus, Minister internal works RepublicBelarus and Minister Board to indicate, to declare security Republic Belarus.

Article 29. Supervision of the implementation of the legislation of the

Republic of Belarus in Turkeysphere fight against corruption

Supervision of correct and uniform implementation of republican legislation It is carried out by the Prosecutor General of Belarus in the field of anti-corruption. faces of Belarus and subordinates he is prosecutors.

EPISODE 7

END REGULATIONS

Matter thirty. Promotion in force to present live

This Law enters into force six months after it becomes official. With the exception of Chapter 7, which entered into force on the date of official publication, publication publications of this Law

Article 31 from the branch hereby live

Council ministers Republic Belarus in Three months term after that entrancein force to present Live:

Presenting the National Assembly of the Republic of Belarus to the Chamber of Deputies Proposals to bring the legislative acts of the Republic of Belarus into compliance with the legislation race with hereby by law;

lead Answers governments Republic Belarus in suitability with over- on foot by law;

to ensure that the state is reviewed and

abolished by the organs of the republic Administration, regulatory, subordinate to the Cabinet of Ministers of the Republic of Belarus legal acts inconsistently to present Live;

to accept other quantity, necessary for application provisions to present Live.

www.ingramcontent.com/pod-product-compliance
Lightning Source LLC
Chambersburg PA
CBHW052342220526
45465CB00003BA/917